This Book was given to "Mum"
in 1994.

Eventually to be passed on to
Martin,

To remind him of a brother who
does
love him,

Blessings to you both
from
Mum.

HOW TO MANAGE YOUR RECORDS

HOW TO
MANAGE YOUR RECORDS

A GUIDE TO EFFECTIVE PRACTICE

EDITED BY

PETER EMMERSON, BA, DAS

Chief Archivist, Barclays Bank PLC

ICSA Publishing

CAMBRIDGE

Published by ICSA Publishing Limited,
Fitzwilliam House, 32 Trumpington Street,
Cambridge CB2 1QY, England

First published 1989

© ICSA Publishing Ltd, 1989

British Library Cataloguing in Publication Data
How to manage your records
1. Records management
I. Emmerson, Peter
651.5

ISBN 0-902197-81-9

Designed by Geoff Green
Typeset by Hands Fotoset, Leicester
Printed in Great Britain by BPCC Wheatons Ltd, Exeter

CONTENTS

ACKNOWLEDGEMENTS

The editor wishes to thank the following organisations for permission to adapt their forms and other documentation as illustrations: the County Archivist, Berkshire County Council; British Steel Corporation; James Martin Associates.

Graham Southwood of the Department of Trade and Industry provided invaluable assistance with Chapter 5.

Thanks are also due to the Chairman and members of the Institute of Chartered Secretaries and Administrators' working party on records management, on whose initiative the project was undertaken, for their consistent support and helpful criticisms.

CONTRIBUTORS

Peter Emmerson is Chief Archivist of Barclays Bank PLC. He was formerly with British Steel (1976–87) where he held senior posts in the Records Services Section, and before that with the National Archives of Rhodesia (now Zimbabwe). A graduate of the University of Rhodesia, he holds a diploma in Archive Studies from the University of London. He is Executive Vice President of the International Records Management Council and former Chairman of the Society of Archivists Records Management Group. He is course director of the Business Archives Council's Introduction to Archives and Records Management and a former lecturer in Archives and Records Management at the Roehampton Institute of Education. He is a frequent speaker on records management topics.

Shelley Hardcastle is a Records Management Consultant with Britannia Data Management PLC. Prior to taking up her present post she was Head of the BBC's Records Management Centre and was responsible for its design and construction. A university graduate, she holds a diploma in Archives from the Roehampton Institute, on which course she subsequently taught. She has lectured in Records Management at University College, London, and is former Chairperson of the Records Management Society.

Carey Moran is Company Records Manager with MEPC PLC and was formerly company Archivist with RTZ PLC. She has considerable experience in the development of computerised records control systems and is an occasional speaker at records management conferences and seminars.

Carl Newton is Director of Strategic Information Management, his own consultancy business. He was formerly County Archivist for

East Sussex and in the business world has held senior records management posts with British Steel and British Petroleum, as Company Records Manager and Records Consultancy Manager. He was subsequently Managing Consultant with James Martin Associates. He holds a degree in Modern History from Oxford and a diploma in Archive Studies from the University of London. He is a member of the Institute of Information Scientists, an associate of the Institute of Management Consultants and a registered member of the Society of Archivists. He was Executive Vice President (Europe) of the International Records Management Council from 1984 to 1988. Carl is a frequent writer and speaker on the strategic aspects of information and records management.

Elizabeth Parker is Manager, Records Management Projects with BP Oil (UK) Ltd. A graduate of the University of Glasgow, she also holds a diploma in Archive Studies from the University of London. She began her career in records management with British Steel in 1979 and was subsequently Records Manager with Berkshire County Council (1983–1986) until taking up her present post. She is Secretary of the Records Management Group of the Society of Archivists and has been heavily involved in the development of the Group's training and seminars programme.

Garry Tapper is a departmental support officer in the Central Government Computing organisation. The last eight of his twenty years in computing have been spent in document imaging systems providing support and advice to departments on microfilm and optical disk systems. He is chairman of the British Standards Committee on document imaging on microfilm and optical disk, and also convenes the International Standards Working Group on legal admissibility. He has been closely involved with the National Centre for Information Media and Technology (CIMTECH) and is a member of the British Computer Society Document Imaging Specialist Group. He lectures widely and contributes to many technical journals.

Other contributors

Michael Cook, MA (Universities) is University Archivist, University of Liverpool.

William Doyle, FCIS (Charities) is clerk to the Governors of the Bishopsgate Foundation.

Alastair King (Charities) is Administrator, Church Pastorial Aid Society.

John Stuttaford (Partnerships) is Partnership Secretary at Banks, Woods and Partners, Quantity Surveyors.

Margaret Whittick (Local Government) is Senior Archivist, Records Management, East Sussex County Council.

INTRODUCTION

THE continuing demand for the Institute of Chartered Secretaries and Administrators booklet, *The Disposal and Retention of Documents* demonstrates the concern felt by its members, and others in the business and government communities over the cost, in particular, of retaining the large quantities of documentation in all formats, produced in the course of modern business. However, the advice given in that slim volume, while generally valuable and accurate, does not go far enough. Because, by its very nature, such a booklet is superficial and general, it cannot begin to address the specific problems of individual businesses. Nor can it deal with the wider philosophical and technical problems of the management of internally generated records and information which exist within those businesses.

All organisations create records in the course of their business. The increasing complexity of that business, combined with increasing regulation, and the consequent need for management control, have led to an exponential growth in the quantity of records generated in the management of that process. Despite the much-vaunted, computer-led, 'paperless revolution' there seems little likelihood in the short- to medium-term, of a sharp reduction in the amount of paper generated by business systems.

There will, of course, be an increasing use of alternative media in the creation and storage of records and information – computer tapes and disks, optical disks, as well as the more established forms of micrographics – which will also need to be managed. The existence of the necessary technology appears to offer a great opportunity to reduce the amount of paper in circulation. Essentially, this has had the effect of postponing the taking of more immediate, effective action to manage records by promising an instantaneous, technological solution. Paper is, after all, only the physical representation of the records explosion. The conversion of those records to an alternative medium does not remove the need to manage them efficiently and effectively. If anything their greater cost and sophistication increase that need. The push for the 'paperless office' also ignored the way that people actually work and their attachment to the hard-copy medium because of its familiarity, portability, flexibility and lack of machine dependence. The paperless office will ultimately be as useful as the paperless bathroom.

The pressure on office space and storage, and their increasing cost, provides a sharper focus to concern about records and to the physical resources consumed by them. Equally important are the hidden costs: staff time spent in filing and retrieving information; the inability to produce the right record at the right time to defend the organisation's interests; management information being slow to appear; and the general commitment of expensive resources to the unstructured creation, management and disposal of records. More than half of all the people employed in modern organisations are involved to some degree in the use, creation and management of internally generated information. Improving their productivity and effectiveness clearly brings immediate benefits to add to those which arise from improved use of physical resources in the way of equipment and space.

This book is aimed at managers at all levels and in all organisations who have responsibility, directly or indirectly, for these resources and sets out to point the way towards realisable improvements. Its main objective is to make managers aware of the problems involved in creating and handling records and information, and the basic techniques and expertise that can be applied in establishing a programme to manage them and in releasing the information they contain for productive use. While it cannot do more than provide a very broad framework of principle and practice, it draws together the collective experience and expertise of some of the country's leading practitioners in the field as a basis on which to develop a more detailed operation and against which to measure the structure and performance of existing records management systems. The advice given, although general, is practical. For example, many of the forms used as illustrations can be adapted for use within any organisation, though clearly they were designed for specific use in those to which they are attributed.

The book sets out to establish the basic principles and techniques involved in the management of records, irrespective of format or medium. It shows how these techniques can be applied in the systems of the future, some of which are with us now, as well as those of the present. These principles and techniques will be equally applicable to the small business and to the large multi-national corporation. It would be impossible and inappropriate for the authors to attempt to provide answers to all the problems faced by individual organisations. Different environments demand different solutions. All we can hope to do is to suggest ways in which those problems might be approached. In the area of records retention, for example, no attempt has been made to provide 'easy' solutions in the way of lists of suggested retention periods which are frequently misleading, soon out of date or, at best, susceptible to misinterpretation. What we have sought to do is to suggest a methodology which will allow each business or authority to determine its own retention needs in the light of the circumstances which, inevitably, apply uniquely to them. This has been supplemented with a chapter which examines the direct concerns of a number of different types of organisation.

In this, as in other specialist professional areas, there is no substitute for the employment of qualified, competent records or information professionals, either directly or as consultants. They will inevitably provide a much more effective answer to an organisation's records and information problems by the application of the principles and techniques described in this book to that organisation's particular circumstances and by taking into account its unique operational, legal and information requirements. The book provides some guidance for the responsible manager in evaluating any proposal which is offered, should such a professional be employed. At the very least it will dispel the simplistic view that records and information management is just a matter of 'filing' which can be delegated to junior staff with impunity. Records and the information they contain are a major business resource. The commitment of adequate physical and personnel resources is essential if it is to be properly managed and exploited and the investment already made in it fully repaid.

The book will supply an overview of some of the legal requirements for records management, but this is by no means a comprehensive study of the legislation. All prices are correct at time of publication and are liable to fluctuate.

CHAPTER 1

WHAT IS RECORDS MANAGEMENT?

PETER EMMERSON

Chief Archivist, Barclays Bank PLC

Introduction

RECORDS management is an administrative system by which an organisation seeks to control the creation, distribution, filing, retrieval, storage and disposal of those records which are created or received by that organisation in the course of its business. In this 'information age', it is also the means by which the valuable information which is contained in those records is released in support of that business.

What records are we talking about?

Records are all those documents, in whatever medium, received or created by an organisation in the course of its business, and retained by that organisation as evidence of its activities or because of the information contained. Records, it must be stressed, are, first and foremost, products of the activities of which they form a part. They arise naturally from the functions, activities, processes and transactions, substantive and facilitative, of the creating organisation. Indeed, records have no existence other than as a product of business activity, without which they have no context or meaning.

The function of records management

The business has a continuing need for these records in two major areas. They are required as evidence of the policies and activities of the business. They demonstrate and confirm the decisions taken by the organisation, the actions carried out in the course of business and the results of those actions. As such they can be produced in court to support legal action and to regulatory authorities to show that regulations are being complied with. From the point of view of the shareholders of a company, or the electorate in the case of central and local government, the availability of records enables them to make an assessment of the stewardship and control undertaken by their elected representatives in the management of the assets placed in their charge and in the carrying out of their statutory duties.

The second area, which is increasingly the more important, is the provision of information for the day-to-day management of the business. It remains a fact that, even in these days of on-line databases and screen-based systems, most of the information required in managing any organisation comes from within its own resources. In a strategic sense, it may be necessary to be aware of the wider information stock relating to the business, requiring access to externally generated data on competitors, markets, regulations and the like but the majority of decisions will be based on analysis of data produced within the host organisation. The raw data of most management information systems is to be found in the records of the business itself. It is, therefore, important for the records needed for such operations to be readily available and clearly identified. Given the contribution they can make to the sound management of the enterprise, the cost of managing them is easily offset. It has been estimated that the cost of filling a single filing cabinet can reach £20,000 per annum. Clearly this money is wasted if the information contained cannot be retrieved or used in the management of the business. By the same token this wastage is compounded if redundant data is retained and stored, in hard copy, on microfilm or magnetically, beyond its useful life.

The format or medium in which the record is held is unimportant to its management. There is a belief that by converting the record to a magnetic medium or reducing it in size by transferring it to microfilm, management has been applied. Nothing could be further from the truth. A messy records system which is reduced or digitised remains a mess and access to it is probably reduced rather than increased. Records in whatever medium need to go through the same decision-making processes to ensure their sensible management. If they are to perform the functions which are required of them they need to be subjected to the same disciplines, irrespective of the medium in which they appear. Unnecessary records are more expensive in digital form than they are on paper and the cost of transferring records to microfilm is an additional expense which should only be entered into after careful consideration and justification. Records management seeks to provide an analytical framework and procedure within which these various alternatives can be sensibly evaluated.

It is true, however, that the sheer volume of records now generated in the course of business has increased enormously even in recent years. The advent of massive record-producing machines in the form of copiers, computers and the like, linked with increased control and regulation, has caused an exponential growth in the quantity of records held in most organisations. The ability to produce records and generate data has been seen as the equivalent of the need to do so. Consequently the physical and human resources consumed in the process have also increased. Identification of the symptoms has led to the desire to achieve 'quick cures' without thinking through the full consequences of the action taken. As with many patent medicines, it is the symptoms rather than the disease which are being treated. There is an assumption that by removing the physical evidence of the records in the form of paper, the problem will be eliminated. If this is done in an unplanned and unmanaged way, the records needed for the efficient and effective operation of the business will be treated in exactly the same way as those of little or no value.

At the same time, excessive retention of records and information can be as dangerous as not retaining enough. An action for discovery of documents in a legal situation, for example, could lead to the obtaining of records which were not strictly relevant to the case but none the less damaging, as well as those which could quite legitimately have been destroyed in the normal course of a managed programme. By the same token, excessive destruction can lead to necessary records not being available when they are required to enable the organisation to defend itself. Either things past and forgotten come back to haunt you or the baby is thrown out with the bathwater. Records management seeks to find a rational compromise between these two extremes.

Of what, then, does records management consist? It is the development of a programme to control records throughout their life from creation to ultimate disposal, either as waste-paper or as an addition to the archives of the creating organisation. The programme should seek to ensure that records and the information and evidence they contain are available to the creating body as a management resource for as long as they are needed and no longer, and that during this time the fullest use can be made of the resource. There is little point in maintaining what is effectively an enormous database if little use is made of it because it is inappropriate to the work carried out by the organisation, or because there are insufficient keys or finding-aids to release the information contained, or if the records cannot be produced in evidence when the need arises. Such occasions may be infrequent but they are usually important. The resources consumed in the creation of records and information are substantial and it therefore makes sense to manage those resources in a sensible way. Few businesses would be as casual over the management of productive resources as they are in respect of the costs of managing records and information. For a relatively small outlay, a number of substantial benefits will accrue.

Benefits of records management

There are a number of benefits which accrue from the establishment of a records management programme. Many of these can be translated into immediately realisable cost savings by the reduction in office space and staff time allocated to records (hard savings). Others make a less direct and readily quantifiable, but equally important, contribution by improving efficiency and effectiveness within the business (soft savings).

Hard savings

These are the most immediate and obvious savings that can be achieved. They relate to the direct application of resources in the form of space, equipment and staff to the management of the records produced and received in the course of business and are consequently those most readily translatable into cash terms.

The physical aspects of managing and storing records are particularly obvious to managers responsible for the provision of office space. Filing cabinets of whatever shape and size require capital expenditure to acquire and generally occupy space in the most expensive part of any building, that occupied by the workers who create and use the records as part of their activities. A standard four-drawer filing cabinet occupies some 8–10 square feet of floor space. That space attracts rental and rates, and has to be serviced, in precisely the same way as the adjacent space occupied by productive individuals. For office accommodation in the City of London, for example, at the time of writing, rent, rates and services combined are in the region of £100 per square foot per annum. A single four-drawer filing cabinet would, therefore, cost up to £1,000 a year in space costs alone before any work was carried out on its contents. Clearly a reduction in the amount of such space occupied by records by the removal of unnecessary holdings must bring quantifiable, if sometimes postponed, benefits to the organisation. These savings are not always immediately realisable unless the space occupied is being reorganised. However, such reorganisation occurs fairly frequently in dynamic environments. At the very least a records management programme will lead to cost avoidance because new accommodation will not have to be provided simply to house redundant records and information. As an additional bonus, the removal of unnecessary filing equipment will improve the working environment for the staff who share the space and thus, in all probability, their productivity.

Equally important, though less easily substantiated and realised, are the savings available from the more sensible application of staff resources. In most large organisations well over half the staff are employed in the creation, filing, manipulation and management of information. Because this involvement is diffuse, it is frequently difficult to quantify accurately. Information and records work is often only a part of a wider activity and a reduction in the time spent on it will, therefore, bring only a marginal improvement or saving in direct employment costs by reducing the number of jobs involved. However, those staff involved will be released to do more productive work if the records and information systems they use and manage are more effective and better organised.

Soft savings

Even more difficult to quantify are the intangible benefits which come from more effective use of the records themselves and of the information they contain. The benefits to management of improved information retrieval cannot be over-estimated. Decision-making may not necessarily be improved by the provision of timely and appropriate data but at least it will be better informed and less open to the challenge of ignorance. Decisions should also be arrived at more quickly because less time will be spent actually searching for the required data. Such improvements in performance and productivity occur at the point in the management pyramid where they are most effective – the manager – rather than the support staff at which most of the improvements in office productivity have so far been aimed.

A sound records management policy and programme will also enable the right document to be produced at the right time in support of the needs of the business in defending itself against attack from its competitors, customers or clients or in supporting its case when it needs to take such action against others. The records which survive as evidence of the activities of the business will be more readily available because the records management programme will ensure that they are more clearly identified. If the organisation should become involved in litigation it will be in a better position to defend itself. Even if the necessary records have not survived, it will be a more satisfactory defence to be able to demonstrate that they were destroyed as part of a planned and managed programme rather than as a result of *ad hoc* action when filing equipment was full or magnetic storage needed to be re-used.

Above all, however, as with any management technique, the most significant benefit will be obtained from the improved control of a valuable resource which is inherent in the development of a records management programme, however limited in scope it may be. Being aware of the size of the problem and having a framework within which it can be managed is a major step in the direction of providing a workable solution to that problem. Similarly, improved performance is bound to arise from knowing what you have in the way of records systems and information resources, identifying what you need and then matching the two to enable them to make the maximum contribution to business effectiveness and efficiency. Because records and information touch every part of the work of an organisation, improvements in the way they are managed can provide equally widespread benefits. The relatively low cost of setting up such a programme will be recovered many times over in the savings which can be achieved.

CHAPTER 2

ESTABLISHING A RECORDS MANAGEMENT POLICY

PETER EMMERSON

A strategy for records management

AS with any other business activity, it is important to devise a strategy for the introduction of records management into an organisation. It must be seen as a means of furthering the aims and objectives of the organisation and as making a direct contribution to the critical success of the business and of the individual departments, functions and components of that business. It is also important that records management should be seen as a dynamic activity which develops along with the business and changes, accommodates and adjusts its aims and objectives accordingly. Experience shows that in organisations where this principle has not been followed, established records management programmes fall by the wayside and the benefits they have achieved are quickly forgotten or taken for granted.

In developing a records management policy and programme it is therefore essential to be aware of what the business or authority that the policy and procedure is designed to serve does, what it sees as its main reason for existing and what it considers to be important in achieving its strategic ends. Any changes in that strategy should be reflected in the records and information systems which are required to support the relevant business activities in carrying out their key tasks. Clearly there will be a difference of emphasis between the approach of a large multinational corporation, operating in a number of different countries and under a number of different legal systems, and that of a small family business with a small number of customers and a relatively straightforward product. Nevertheless, it is imperative that the records manager, or the person responsible for the programme and policy, should be aware of the strategic framework within which it will operate.

There are many questions which need to be asked and answered to ensure that the policy determined and the programme set up make a direct contribution to the achievement of the strategic goals of the wider organisation. It is also important that the records management operation itself has a clear set of strategic goals which match those of the organisation, against which it can measure its achievements and within which it can determine the resources that it needs. The whole question of strategic development of records and information management is dealt with at greater length by Carl Newton in Chapter 7, 'The future of records management', but it needs to be stressed that such an approach is essential if any programme introduced is to enjoy long-term success and maintain its relevance to the organisation.

Before beginning to establish a policy or programme, the responsible manager needs to establish very clearly the environment in which the policy will be introduced and to plan at a tactical level too. Again, a number of questions need to be asked and answered. How great is the demand for live information? To what extent does storage or volume dominate the thinking of the organisation in its approach to the management of its records? Is the inability to produce the right record at the right time likely to cost the organisation substantial loss, either financially or in terms of reputation? How is the organisation structured and how will this influence the way records management might be introduced? (Highly decentralised organisations may prove more difficult to influence than those which are accustomed to central control.) What is the organisational culture and how receptive will it be to a new set of guidelines or instructions on any subject? How much selling is going to be necessary to get the programme and policy accepted and which route should be followed in seeking acceptance? What kind of records management arrangements exist at present (there are bound to be some, however unsophisticated)? Are they seen as effective and who is responsible for them? What resistance will be put forward by those who see their territory being impinged upon in the organisation as a whole or within individual departments?

Records management policy

For records management to succeed, a clear and comprehensive policy must be laid down which is known to have high-level support within the organisation. This should establish the status of the policy and programme within the business, its aims and objectives, the responsibility of individuals in relation to the implementation of the policy and the carrying out of the programme. The policy may be very broad in the form of a statement of intent, or very detailed as a set of precise instructions encapsulated in a detailed manual or handbook to which all records management activities should conform. In general, the style will usually depend on the type of organisation in which the policy is being introduced. It has to be said, however, that a high degree of decentralisation, at least in the control of a records management programme, is incompatible with the success of such a policy. Some monitoring from the centre is essential to ensure that it works well and effectively.

Establishing the status of the policy is an essential ingredient in any successful records and information programme. Although it should not be necessary to fall back on, for example, the stated support of the managing director or chief executive, the ability to use the existence of high-level support when initiating a programme is a major advantage. Certainly it may be difficult to overcome resistance or gain co-operation for what, on the surface, may seem to be another bureaucratic irrelevance, unless the policy is clearly supported and officially promulgated. Thereafter, however, it is up to the person managing the programme to ensure that it makes a full contribution to the working needs of the people most directly affected – the creators and users of the records and information.

Aims of a records management policy

What should the aims of such a policy be? Simply, to improve the quality of records and information management in line with the organisation's established needs and critical success factors. It can be expressed in terms of a need to contain costs, to reduce paper holdings, to produce fewer but better records or to provide a fully integrated records and information management system, with full applicability across the organisation and linked to the introduction of, say, an office automation programme. Whatever that aim is, it should encapsulate as far as possible the essence of the policy agreed by management.

Objectives of a records management policy

Detailed objectives for the policy and programme should be established at this point in order to make it clear precisely what needs to be done to give shape to the broad aim of the policy. The development of procedures and systems to give effect to the broad policy fall within this area and they provide the milestones against which to measure progress towards the overall policy goals as well as providing the framework for the programme. They define the scope of the various programme elements and establish the full range of the agreed programme. They may include, for example, the following objectives:

1. To establish records control systems.
2. To improve information retrieval from records by improving classification and indexing systems and introducing the use of information technology.
3. To establish a retention control system for records with the development, following analysis, of retention schedules covering all records in use within the organisation.
4. To develop rules throughout the organisation for the preparation of file titles.
5. To develop a system for the management of special reports.
6. To make recommendations for the development of storage facilities.
7. To establish a system for controlling the design and development of forms.
8. To identify those records which are vital to the survival of the organisation and arrange for them to be suitably protected.
9. To investigate and recommend on the conversion of records to alternative media.
10. To establish rules for the management and control of records held in machine-readable form.
11. To include these and other detailed procedures in a comprehensive manual.

The objectives set will naturally depend on the overall scope of the policy which has been negotiated and on the resources made available. These in turn will be based on the perceived needs of the organisation and may well have to be built up over a period of time in a series of incremental developments as the value of the programme becomes more clearly established. This should not deter the records manager from setting clear objectives in pursuit of the overall strategy. However, he should have a clear view of what minimum achievements are possible within the available resources and where the greatest impact is likely to be made (see Fig. 2.1).

Records management policy

Definitions

RECORDS MANAGEMENT: Will ensure that the company retains (and increasingly creates) only those records which it requires to conduct its business; that those which are created are managed and controlled effectively and at the least cost, commensurate with operational and information needs.

RECORDS: Any paper, book, photograph, microfilm, map, drawing, chart, magnetic tape or disk (or any copy of print-out thereof), or optical disk, that has been generated or received by an organisation and has been used by that organisation or its successors as evidence or because of the information contained.

Aims

To improve the management of the company's records and to enhance their use as an information resource.

Objectives

To ensure:

1. that records, or the information they contain, can be retrieved accurately and quickly to aid decision-making and increase management effectiveness;
2. that records created in the course of business are retained for the minimum period of time;
3. that those records retained beyond immediate operational needs are stored cheaply and retrieved effectively when needed, reviewed regularly and disposed of promptly;
4. that total resources applied to the management of records at all levels are reduced and that those resources are more productively used;
5. that records are handled in the medium most appropriate for the task they perform; and
6. that those records worth retaining permanently, because of their administrative, organisational or informational value (archives) are identified at the earliest possible moment.

Methodology

1. Analyse record holdings and systems to produce agreed retention periods for all series of records.
2. Codify this data into departmental records retention authorities and schedules.
3. Destroy all time-expired records.
4. Immediately transfer non-current records to low-cost, high-density storage facilities (e.g. Central Records Store).
5. Advise on improvements in current records systems to suit departmental and corporate needs.
6. Assess existing records systems for conversion to alternative media (microfilm, computers, optical disk, etc.).
7. Apply information technology to the management of current and non-current records.

Fig. 2.1 A typical records management policy.

Responsibility under the policy

The policy document should as far as possible identify the person with overall responsibility for the policy and what the levels of delegated responsibility are. There is a natural logic in the records manager being responsible for ensuring that all aspects of the policy are in fact carried out, either by direct line responsibility for the necessary facilities and for the staff who are involved in records management work, or by being functionally responsible for monitoring the work done by staff who are line-responsible to other managers. Either of these approaches will work given the right policy structure and provided there is a willingness to co-operate. Whatever the specific arrangements in detail, it will always be necessary to provide for the monitoring, as a matter of routine, of the consistent application of the policy. This can best be achieved by way of regular contact between the records management department and staff of the relevant operational unit, or through the co-operation of the equivalent of an internal audit or inspection department. Without consistent and regular monitoring it is all too easy for established standards to begin to slip and for the policy and programme to fall into disuse.

The role of the records manager

The records manager plays a key role in both the development of a records management policy and its implementation. It is, therefore, vital to ensure that the right person is selected and that they are suitably trained and fully aware of the requirements of the job. An appointment to the most senior post in a records management section requires someone who has the detailed understanding, professionalism and experience to generate confidence that they know what they are doing in this specialist field. An awareness of records, and the way they are created and function, is an essential prerequisite. Increasingly, too, the records manager will also require a wider knowledge of the development of systems for the provision of information and of the technology which can be specifically applied to the management of records and information. On a more personal level the records manager should also have the necessary qualities and authority to communicate confidently at all levels from senior management downwards, both face-to-face and in writing. The ability to plan comprehensively and flexibly to meet the requirements of the organisation is a must, as is the capacity to relate to the requirements and constraints of the business. In short, this is an appointment for an experienced practitioner, not for an inexperienced, first-time appointee. The making of a low-level appointment in the hope of saving money will probably prove counter-productive.

The management of information resources is gaining growing recognition as a vital part of the management of any business. There is a demand for relevant information to be delivered more rapidly to the decision-makers which makes the role of the information manager and provider more important than ever. It is particularly important, therefore, to ensure that fully trained records and information professionals are used to carry out this task. Awareness of the problems on the part of other professionals does not necessarily mean an equal awareness of the answers.

What, then, is the role of the records manager once an appointment has been made? The records manager should be responsible to a senior executive for all aspects of records management. At the very least, he or she should be available to advise on the establishment of records management policy and to develop standards for the management of records across the organisation. In decentralised organisations, this control may be all that is possible, but as a minimum it should be supported with a degree of monitoring which goes beyond that of an occasional report. If that level of central control does not exist then it is unlikely that the policy can be made to work satisfactorily.

Functional responsibility without any degree of authority means that control will be dependent on the personal reputation and persuasive skills of the individual records manager, thus increasing the need for someone whose credibility is well-established. Ideally the records manager should be in a position, as the leading professional, to initiate, control and implement the programmes and systems which go into making up records management as it has been set out briefly above, and which will be described in more detail in the following chapters. After all, the records manager is the one professional individual in the organisation who is interested in the total corporate information and documentary stock, and whose training and experience is specifically geared towards the management of this resource. Few organisations would employ a lawyer to manage their accounts department. It is equally important to employ professionals in this area too, certainly to set up the systems in the first place, because they are more likely to get them up and running in the shortest possible time.

Selection and training of records management staff

The records manager should also be involved in the selection of

staff to be employed directly in records management, either by
specifically recruiting them or in designing the necessary jobs and
writing the job descriptions. Records and information work is
fundamental to the well-being of the organisation and it is
important that the jobs are properly structured and suitably
rewarded to attract the right kind of people. The records manager
should also be responsible for the continuing training and
education, through courses, seminars, individual tuition and
periods of attachment, of those involved both directly and
indirectly in records and information work. This will ensure that
they are kept up to date with the latest developments and that their
skills are maintained in a changing environment. It will also help to
provide continuity as inevitable staff changes take place. Standards
of service and operation will thus be maintained and, where
possible, improved.

In the past, records work has been seen as, at best, a route to
another post in the organisation. It has been characterised as boring
and contributing little to the general well-being of the business.
Given the real importance of the sound management of internally
generated information, it is imperative to change this view and to
encourage those who enter records work to see it as being a vital,
integrated part of the organisational structure. To this end, the
creation of a records management department with its own career
structure can be beneficial, in that it raises the profile of the work
and makes it appear more attractive to brighter entrants. Too often
records work has been, and still is, seen as the lowest level of clerical
task, an attitude which goes a long way to explaining the poor
quality of many records systems and the problems which have
arisen. Although the routine activities involved in records management may appear less than exciting, their placement within a wider
structure makes it possible to devise a more interesting approach to
information work than might otherwise be the case. The presence,
too, of dedicated and enthusiastic professional management can
make a substantial impact on the way in which subordinate and
support staff respond to the job in hand. A typical records
management operation would include posts in analysis and systems
design, records administration (providing filing services and
managing records centre facilities, for example), micrographics,
etc. at both the professional/managerial level and at the level of
clerical and support staff. Given proper training and extension
facilities, there should be ample opportunity for a career to be built
in this area on its own. At the same time the skills acquired and the
knowledge of the business which records and information staff
develop should also open up other areas of opportunity. In no

sense, however, should the value to the organisation of records and information work be underestimated and under-regarded.

Further developments

Once the initial setting-up process has been carried through, it may be possible to devolve operational responsibility for records management to local control. However, the records manager would need to retain responsibility for the maintenance of the retention system and centralised physical storage facilities, and for the monitoring of departmental systems to ensure that they remain relevant and up to date. The records manager should also provide a focal point of knowledge and interest to enable new developments to be assessed and to which operational units could turn with their problems and requirements. If this course is followed, it is still important to retain the interest of records management staff and to ensure that they are adequately trained. Local changes in methodology and approaches to record-keeping should also be considered carefully before implementation in order to maintain consistency. However, if local management are prepared to accept full accountability for any failure, they should be allowed to develop systems and operations to suit their local needs. Consultation with the records manager would obviate the worst consequences of this approach and lead to the development of systems which are both consistent with policy and responsive to local needs – a position which should in fact be the basis of any good records or information system.

Qualifications for a records manager

There are few formal qualifications available for records managers in the United Kingdom. Most of those practising have received their training in one or more of the standard information disciplines, archive administration, librarianship or information science. Of these only the postgraduate archive courses have offered records management either as a specific part of an integrated course or as a compulsory core subject in those courses where options are offered.

The profession recognises the importance of sound records control in ensuring that suitable records survive the disposal process to become archives. Consequently archivists have been responsible for the development of a core of records management theory and practice in the United Kingdom and, indeed, in other parts of the world, and for the introduction of the concept to the thinking of managers in business and in central and local government. This is hardly surprising as archivists are the only information professionals who have original records as the basis for their work.

Concern for the management of records in the latter part of the life-cycle has led to a natural movement of interest back along the chronological chain. The relationship of the archivist with records management has therefore been a close one, particularly in the public sector. The basic training that archivists receive on the nature of records and the organisations which create them is of great value in carrying out records management tasks. However, it has to be said that the training they receive has probably not kept pace with the changing needs of records management today.

Increasingly, with the growing importance of information provision in modern management and administration, a wider spread of information and management services professionals has become interested and involved. Those skilled in indexing and in the organisation of current information from printed sources have become more directly associated with the management of internally generated information and therefore with the records in which it is contained, as well as in the books, serials and databases which they have traditionally used. The transition is not an easy one. Records have a unique quality which is missing from printed materials. They are a natural organic growth from business activity and have an evidential quality as well as being a source of information. As will be demonstrated in later chapters of this book, an awareness of this fact is crucial to the success of any records management scheme. Any attempt to produce a programme based on information content alone will be disastrous.

Nevertheless, converging technologies have led to an increasing need for all records managers, whatever their background, to address the problems of delivering the information contained in records at the point of demand. The user of live information is largely unconcerned about its source, and is interested only in its accuracy and the speed at which it is delivered. An increasingly common approach will be needed by all the information professions which will match and make use of the technology that so dominates the planning for information provision. At the very least any records manager approaching a new project should be able to demonstrate an awareness of this 'seamlessness' and an understanding of the skills and philosophies of fellow professionals.

Because there is no specific qualification for records managers in this country, the main associations involved – the Society of Archivists Records Management Group, the Records Management

Society, ASLIB and the Business Archives Council – all provide training for their own members in specific skills and run seminars to introduce records management to others. They also seek to discuss with related professions their areas of common interest and to make them aware of the things that make records unique from other information-carrying documents. Any of these organisations will be happy to advise on the appointment of records managers.

With this essential philosophical grounding in the nature of records, however, and an awareness of the various elements involved, any trained information professional should be able to master the basics of a records management programme. Essentially the methods used are those which apply to any management task, investigation and analysis and the implementation of these into a workable scheme. Above all, the records manager should be clear-thinking, methodical, persuasive, business-orientated, and a good communicator, aware of the developments in technology and above all of the needs of the employing organisation. The records manager's activity and responsibility touch every person in the organisation and reach every corner. The importance to the organisation of its own information gives the records manager a value (largely unrecognised and unrewarded) which is difficult to overestimate.

The use of consultants

Because there is a general shortage of suitably qualified people in the field, there is a steadily growing number of consultants available to provide advice to organisations on the development of records and information management. Many of these consultants are experienced, senior members of the profession who have decided to put their experience to better use on their own behalf and who work as small independent operators. Others are employed by commercial storage organisations, so that those companies can provide a wider professional management service to their clients. In addition, a number of the management consultancy arms of the large accountancy practices have added information and records management to their consultancy portfolios. The existence of this alternative to direct employment, particularly when there is a shortage of high-calibre senior professionals, provides organisations with a viable option in the development of complete records management programmes, in the more rapid completion of various aspects of an in-house programme or, perhaps, in the provision of a training programme for departmental staff.

The decision to use a consultant in this field is governed by the same criteria and rules as would apply in any other. The organisation chosen must be able to demonstrate the expertise and experience required and have the necessary credibility. What have they done before and what was the response of those for whom contracts have been undertaken in the past? Are the ideas and solutions being put forward an answer to the problems of your organisation or those of the previous client? How closely can you specify what it is that you require? Who will be responsible for maintenance of the recommended system? How independent are the consultants in the selection of the systems and technology they recommend?

There are some advantages in using suitably qualified consultants. The work can usually be done faster than in-house and generally at a known, though probably higher, cost. Consultants also have access to the latest techniques and thinking in the field and can bring to bear the experience gained in solving problems elsewhere. Inside the organisation, too, their recommendations frequently carry more weight than those of in-house staff, because they are seen to be outsiders with no particular axe to grind.

However, there are a number of disadvantages which are often the 'flip-side' of the advantages outlined. The very speed with which the work needs to be done to keep the cost within reasonable bounds means that the consultant does not have time to find out as much about the organisation as in-house staff. In records analysis and development, this lack of knowledge can be crucial. There is always a concern that the application of experience gained elsewhere to a new problem means that the consultant is providing a solution to a problem that you do not have – in other words, giving you what you want rather than what you need. The consultant does not have to maintain the system which he sets up. We are all aware of the frequency with which one set of consultants has to be used to sort out the problems created by another. New thinking may also lead to 'flavour of the month' solutions which are not yet sufficiently tried and tested and which subsequently fail.

As long as these reservations are borne in mind, however, and provided that the consultant has satisfactory credentials to undertake the task in hand and the client is in a position to specify that task fairly closely, the use of consultants may well be the best way of introducing or speeding up the introduction of records management into an organisation. As always, much will depend on the circumstances in which the work is to be done. The ideal solution may well be to use consultants to undertake the non-repetitive work but under the control of an in-house records manager who will then be responsible for the maintenance of the system which subsequently emerges. A number of large organisations in the United Kingdom have established what are, in effect, in-house consultancy units which would seem to provide the best of both worlds. If no in-house expertise exists, any scheme proposed should be evaluated in the light of the principles and procedures which are set out in the following chapters.

Whatever course of action is chosen and however simple or comprehensive the approach, it is important to persevere with the records management programme to obtain the benefits which have been outlined above. There are no simple solutions. It may be possible to speed up the process by committing the necessary resources within a shorter timescale and thereby increasing the short-term costs, but it will not be possible to avoid the work which needs to be done. However, the deliverable results of the programme in both improved resource utilisation and information provision will more than repay the effort and investment.

CHAPTER 3

DEVELOPING THE PROGRAMME

ELIZABETH A. PARKER

Manager, Records Management Projects, BP Oil (UK) Limited

The framework of the programme

EFFECTIVE development of the records management programme, as with any aspect of business, requires the establishment of a management framework and an operational methodology. The essential first step in providing the management framework is, as has been suggested, the appointment of a manager with overall responsibility for the programme. This appointment must be at a sufficiently senior level in the organisation to provide strategic management for the programme. Ideally the appointee should be a professional records manager. However, this is not essential provided that someone with professional records management expertise is involved at an appropriate level to direct and control the technical quality of the programme.

Following the allocation of overall responsibility, it is vital to establish the involvement of management from all areas of the organisation in order to ensure that, from the outset, the programme is relevant and responsive to business needs. This is most effectively achieved by the nomination of a manager from each area to act as programme co-ordinator for that area. Formal terms of reference should be defined and a communication structure established for the programme manager and the area co-ordinators to ensure that up-to-date progress information is regularly and appropriately disseminated throughout the organisation. Opposition or resistance can also be formally addressed and resolved within this same framework.

Methodology

Having set up the management framework for the programme, the operational methodology can be established. This is achieved through the production of a strategic business plan defining the scope, aims and objectives of the programme and outlining a proposed development schedule with appropriate cost-benefit projections. This plan can be produced either by the programme manager for approval by the programme co-ordinators or by a joint working party led by the programme manager.

To define the scope, aims and objectives of the programme, the programme manager needs to establish an overview of the following:

(a) organisational structure;
(b) business functions;
(c) business imperatives and priorities, e.g. profit, public image;
(d) records management systems and practices;
(e) records management imperatives and priorities, e.g. control, cost, information provision; and
(f) organisational constraints, e.g. structure, cost, development plans.

The data required may be obtained either directly or indirectly (see below) but the best results are achieved by a combination of:

(a) independent research to obtain organisation charts, personnel directories, annual reports, business plans, etc.;
(b) discussion with programme co-ordinators, and other personnel as appropriate, regarding operation and planned development of business functions and the existing and desired state of records management, to highlight areas of particular concern or priority; and
(c) a 'walk-through' survey to establish the nature and scale of existing record holdings.

It is particularly important at this stage to establish the existence of any organisational policy and procedure in relation to any aspect of records management, and to identify where responsibility lies for its management and operation.

The scope of the programme should be defined in terms of business functions, organisational areas and physical locations as appropriate. A decision must be made at this stage as to whether the programme is to be developed across the entire organisation from the outset or whether one part of the organisation is to be selected as the subject of a pilot study for subsequent extension to other parts on the basis of defined criteria. This decision must be based on individual organisational circumstances, taking into account all relevant factors such as cost, management support and organisational culture. It may be necessary or appropriate to produce plans for both approaches to enable comparative cost-benefit assessments to be made.

Within the defined scope, the aims of the programme must be set up in relation to the business, i.e. what business benefits are sought or anticipated from the programme. The objectives for the programme should be specified in terms of records management modules, for example classification, media conversion, vital records protection, retention, storage and exploitation. These objectives must be realistically achievable in the context of the organisation and its business, and specific criteria should be established, as far as possible, for measurement of their achievement. Examples of well-structured objectives for a records management programme include: to cut the costs of intermediate storage for records by 20 per cent over five years; to improve classification of records in order to cut the 'turn-round' time on information retrieval requests to a maximum of twenty minutes.

The development schedule

A development schedule can only be planned when the scope, aims and objectives have been defined. The schedule should set out the content, sequence, timing and resourcing of the work involved in the development of the programme. The content of the work will be determined by the application of records management principles and practice to the specified objectives of the programme and it should be planned on a project basis involving the following discrete phases of activity to maintain control in terms of relevance to the objectives and integration of the various modules of the programme:

Phase I   Data collection
Phase II   Analysis/specification
Phase III   Design
Phase IV   Implementation

The sequence of work should be defined in terms of dependent and independent objectives, as it may be necessary or desirable to vary the pace of development on different modules. The timing of the work should be calculated in working-days for translation into 'real-time', taking into account all known constraints; 'hard' estimates of timescale should be provided for Phase I, based on a detailed work plan, with 'soft' estimates for Phases II–IV, based on outline work plans, for revision at the start of each phase when more detailed versions will be drawn up. 'Hard' estimates of requirements for personnel (indicating quantity *and* quality), money and other resources should be provided for all phases of the development work, with an indication of the timing of each of these requirements and responsibility for their provision and control. The schedule should also define the level, extent and nature of 'user participation' which is required in each phase, particularly for approval and authorisation purposes, in order to manage the expectations of the areas which are involved and to ensure that the appropriate personnel can be made available when required to avoid delay and minimise disruption.

Cost-benefit projections must be based on organisational priorities for the business and for records management, and must be realistic and directly relevant to the organisation if they are to have the maximum impact. All pertinent cost factors, both fixed and variable, must be taken into account (personnel, services, equipment, accommodation, etc.).

Following the production of the strategic business plan, the programme manager should determine the appropriate channels and procedures for its approval and dissemination. It is essential that approval of the plan is obtained at a sufficiently senior level in the organisation to ensure that the required management commitment and support for the programme will be forthcoming from the areas which are involved. It is equally important that, once approved, selected information from the plan is appropriately disseminated throughout the organisation, to ensure that personnel at all levels are aware of the programme and its purpose, and of the nature and planned timing of its development, particularly in terms of the 'user participation' which is required. The initial development process will inevitably cause some disruption of normal operations and staff must be made aware of the importance and priority which management attach to the programme and that their co-operation is expected. The completion of appropriate approval and communication of the plan is essential prior to starting development work.

Phase I: Data collection

The objective of this phase is to collect detailed data on the following functions and answer specific questions as a basis for analysis of existing provisions and requirements for the production of a programme specification.

1. Business functions, activities and transactions: What is the organisation's business? How is it conducted? Where, when, why and by whom?

2. Business imperatives: What are the organisation's 'critical success factors'? What is the organisational ethos?
3. Records and records management systems requirements: What records does the organisation require to conduct its business efficiently, effectively and legally and to protect its own interests and those of its employees, the public and others, for example shareholders? Where are the records required for use? When, why and by whom? What are the requirements for storage and disposal? Where, when, why and by whom?
4. Existing records and records management systems: What records are created? How are they created, used, stored and disposed of? Where, when, why and by whom?

The following data are the minimum required for each records series.

(A records series consists of records which arise from the same system, relate to a specific function, activity or transaction, are arranged in a single sequence – numerical, alphabetical or chronological or a combination of these – and which may have the same physical form. A series may be a single volume, a number of files or thousands of individual documents.)

1. The title.
2. The purpose and content in relation to business function, activity or transaction.
3. The record's provenance.
4. Organisational 'history', e.g. department/unit/section.
5. Its status and relationship to other records series: 'greater/less than' and 'equivalent to' relationships, 'original' and 'duplicate', 'prime' and 'non-prime'.
6. The medium, e.g. paper/microform/magnetic.
7. The format such as:
   (a) paper – A4/foolscap, file/book;
   (b) microform – roll/fiche, file/cassette; or
   (c) magnetic – tape/disk, cassette/disk-pack.
8. The arrangement of the record into:
   (a) classification, e.g. function/subject;
   (b) referencing, e.g. alphabetic/numeric; or
   (c) indexing, e.g. subject/keyword.
9. The frequency of creation, e.g. daily/weekly/monthly/quarterly/annually.
10. The period and pattern of use, i.e.:
    (a) time, e.g. day/week/month/quarter/year; and
    (b) purpose, e.g. reference/amendment/update.
11. The period and reason for retention:

(a) time, e.g. current month + 2 months/current year + 1 year; and

(b) purpose, e.g. information/legal or audit requirement.

12. Storage needs:

(a) stationery, e.g. folder, suspension sling, binder; and

(b) equipment, e.g. vertical/lateral cabinet, index drawer, plan chest.

13. The volume of records described in terms of linear or cubic measurement.

14. The date.

15. The location of records in relation to period and pattern of retention, e.g. office for current year + 1 year for information, then storage for 5 years for legal requirements.

Additional data may be required depending on the objectives of the programme. For example, if it is planned to develop a media conversion module, it is necessary to collect data to aid subsequent assessment of potential for conversion, such as background colour of documents and density of images.

The data required may be collected by either direct or indirect methods. Direct methods involve personal contact with departmental personnel and physical examination of records by project staff. Indirect methods involve distribution of forms or questionnaires for completion by departmental personnel.

Direct methods provide a high level of control and flexibility, facilitating the collection of accurate and relevant data with the minimum of disruptive imposition on business operations. Personal contact provides opportunities to market the programme and to identify allies, as well as to deal immediately and constructively with opposition or resistance. The principal disadvantage of these methods is that they are time-consuming, as only a limited number of areas can be dealt with at one time.

Indirect methods lack control and flexibility. While the imposition of the bulk of the work on departmental staff has potential advantages because they will be more familiar with their operations and records, it also creates considerable potential for unnecessary disruption of normal operations, as well as for delay and provision of inaccurate, inconsistent and irrelevant data. Lack of personal contact denies opportunities to deal immediately and constructively with opposition or resistance, increasing the chances for misunderstanding and, possibly, resentment on the part of departmental staff. Meetings with key staff prior to distribution of forms or questionnaires, to explain their purpose and answer questions, may eliminate these problems. The principal advantage of these methods is speed, as all areas of the organisation can be dealt with simultaneously.

The use of direct methods is preferable wherever feasible. The programme is likely to be regarded as having a higher priority and overall as being less time-consuming. Indirect methods may provide short-term benefits, particularly in terms of timescale, but ultimately are likely to prove to be more time-consuming and less effective in terms of both the quality and quantity of data collected. Whatever methods are used, the collection and processing of the data may be facilitated by the use of standard formats. The best results are obtained by using two complementary techniques: interviews of departmental staff and inventory of records.

Interview

Staff should be selected for interview on the basis of their knowledge and experience of the appropriate part of the organisation and its business rather than because of their status within it. With the aim of obtaining required data which cannot be elicited by examination of the records, specific objectives should be drawn up for each interview, tailored to the expected scope of knowledge of the interviewee. In conducting the interviews, it is important to maintain a balance between following a predetermined structure to ensure that all planned lines of inquiry are covered, and remaining sufficiently flexible to follow relevant lines of inquiry which arise unexpectedly in the course of the interview, while not doggedly pursuing those which turn out to be unproductive. The use of a standard form to record data obtained in interviews can be helpful, provided that it incorporates sufficient flexibility for interpretation on the part of the interviewer (see Fig. 3.1). If specific documentation (for example, organisation charts, business plans, operational procedures, standards manuals) is referred to in the course of interviews, copies or examples should be obtained wherever possible.

Inventory

The coverage of the records inventory should be comprehensive, taking in all records in existence, regardless of location, function, medium, format or age. The objective is to obtain as much of the required data as possible through physical examination of individual records series. The best results are obtained by beginning the inventory in locations where records are active. Project staff can then familiarise themselves with the relevant business function and

RECORDS AND MANAGEMENT PROGRAMME

DATA COLLECTION

INTERVIEW SHEET

A   BUSINESS NEEDS

1. What is the function of this area of the business?

2. What activities and transactions are carried out within the area in order to fulfil this function?

3. How are these activities and transactions carried out?

   - Why?

   - Where?

   - By whom?

4. Does this area have relationships with other parts of the organisation?

   - Which areas?

   - Why?

   - What is the nature of the relationship?

   - Who initiates the interaction?

   - When and how?

5. Does the area have working relationships with agencies or individuals outside the organisation?

   - Which agencies or individuals?

   - What is the nature of the relationship?

   - Who initiates interaction?

   - When and how?

B   EXISTING RECORDS SYSTEMS AND PRACTICES

1. How important are records in general to the successful operation of the area?

   - Why?

   - Are any records particularly important?

   - Which records and why?

2. Who is responsible for the management of the records which are created, received and used within the area?

   - for the design, development, implementation and maintenance of the records systems?

3. How long have the currently operating records systems been in place?

4. Do these systems meet current requirements?

   - Why/why not?

5. What changes could be made to the these systems to improve their performance?

Fig. 3.1: A standard interview data record form.

its records in a dynamic environment where, if necessary, they can easily draw on the knowledge and expertise of local staff. This simplifies the inventory process in locations where records are inactive by minimising the need to return to the creating department for further assistance. The use of a standard form (Fig. 3.2) to record data on each records series is essential to ensure consistency. If records series consist of, or are based on, standard forms or formats (for example minutes, reports, manuals), copies or examples should be obtained wherever possible.

RECORDS INVENTORY					
DEPARTMENT		SECTION		UNIT	
TITLE					REF.
DESCRIPTION					
STATUS ORIGINAL ☐ DUPLICATE ☐			PRIMACY PRIME ☐ NON-PRIME ☐		
MEDIUM/FORMAT			ARRANGEMENT		
PAPER ☐:					
MICROFILM ☐:					
MAGNETIC ☐:					
OTHER ☐:					
ACTIVITY/USE			RETENTION		
LOCATION	STATIONERY	EQUITMENT	DATE	VOLUME	NOTES

Fig. 3.2:   Records inventory form.

Unless the organisational culture indicates otherwise, the overall scope of the programme should be subdivided into its organisational components and a 'top-down' approach adopted to the data collection exercise, to enable detailed data to be reconciled within a broader picture. Collection, collation and reconciliation of data must proceed simultaneously in order to ensure that all areas are covered and all inconsistencies are resolved, particularly in terms of linking complementary data from the interview and inventory processes. Working exceptions to this approach may be necessary to avoid delay or unnecessary disruption, for example in areas with unpredictable workloads or where a substantial number of staff are outposted, home-based or absent for long periods. Flexibility is essential to the success of a data collection exercise.

Phase II: Analysis/specification

The objective of this phase is to define and analyse the following individually, and in relation to each other and professional records management methodology, in order to produce a specification for the programme which meets the aims and objectives as approved in the strategic business plan:

(a) business functions, activities and transactions;
(b) existing records and records management systems; and
(c) records and records management systems requirements;

The process of definition and analysis consists of two distinct components:

1. Definition of business functions, activities and transactions, with related records and records management systems, both existing and required.
2. Comparison of existing and required records and records management systems in terms of business needs and professional records management methodology.

The process should be carried out within a predetermined structure to ensure consistency and completeness of coverage. A wide range of analytical techniques is available from the fields of business management and of information systems development. In determining the most appropriate techniques, it is advisable to draw on all available expertise. Within the organisation, there may be established or preferred techniques, for example within organisation and methods, information technology and internal audit departments. Externally, advice and ideas can be obtained from professional organisations and consultants and it can also be useful to draw on the experience of other organisations which have undertaken similar exercises. Whatever techniques are selected, the process cannot be effectively undertaken in isolation. Constant communication with departmental staff is essential to ensure that assumptions are confirmed and misunderstandings eliminated. It is therefore important to consider the amount of translation which is needed to make the results of the process meaningful to non-technical staff, maintaining an appropriate balance between technicality and simplicity. Techniques involving diagrammatic presentations of data are particularly effective, being less cumbersome and more readily comprehensible than detailed textual explanations.

Records management systems should be defined and analysed in terms of intellectual and physical control and exploitation of records.

Intellectual control

This relates to the creation, organisation, classification, storage, retrieval, retention and disposal of records:

1. Whether 'birth control' is practised in relation to the creation of 'new' records, e.g. forms, reports.
2. Whether records are arranged and, if appropriate, classified to reflect the business functions, activities and transactions.
3. Whether systems of arrangement and classification are monitored, controlled and documented.
4. Whether the storage and retrieval of records is monitored, controlled and documented.
5. Whether the retention and disposal of records is monitored, controlled and documented.

Physical control

This also relates to the storage, retrieval and disposal of records:

1. Whether file management procedures are carried out regularly.
2. Whether records are stored in equipment (i.e. stationery and 'furniture') which is appropriate to their medium and format.
3. Whether records are stored in equipment and in an environment which affords adequate (defined by assessment of relative importance to the business) protection from the hazards to which they might be exposed, both human and environmental.
4. Whether records are stored in locations appropriate to their position in the life-cycle, i.e. active records held close to where they are used, inactive records held remotely.
5. Whether records are retained in the most appropriate medium and format for use.
6. Whether records are disposed of by methods appropriate to their format, the medium in which they are held and their security status.

Exploitation

This relates to the value of availability of records as organisational resources:

1. Whether records are created, used and retained for 'information' as well as for evidential purposes.
2. Whether information about the existence of all records and their content is available to all departmental staff.

3. Whether records are available for use by departmental staff other than those directly involved in their creation, use or retention.

A work plan of draft–discuss–revise–finalise should be carried out using a 'top-down' approach similar to that adopted for the data collection exercise, to ensure that all inconsistencies are resolved and inaccuracies eliminated prior to drawing firm conclusions on the distinction between existing and required records and records management systems as the basis for production of the specification for the programme.

The specification should define the systems required for each module of the programme and those required to link related modules to resolve this distinction and to satisfy the aims and objectives of the programme as a whole. It should define the systems in terms of their required content in relation to intellectual and physical control and exploitation of records. A further work plan of draft–discuss–revise–finalise should begin with a 'logical' specification for the 'ideal' programme, taking into account fixed constraints such as organisational structure and culture, internal standards and procedures for related activities, professional records management methodology, legal and other regulatory requirements and existing records management systems. This should then be developed into a 'practical' specification by incorporating known variable constraints such as time, money and personnel and a comparison of the 'logical' and the 'practical' specifications drawn up to identify expected gain/loss of performance due to variable constraints.

The production and presentation of the specifications should take account of the organisational culture and any house style. It may be necessary or appropriate to produce draft specifications for individual modules for discussion and informal approval at various levels before presenting the final integrated version for formal authorisation at the appropriate level as the essential prerequisite of, and starting-point for, work on the design of the individual programme modules.

Phase III: Design

The objective of this phase is to design the systems required for each module of the programme and those required to link related modules as defined in the specification for the programme to meet the aims and objectives as approved in the strategic business plan.

The design of each system must include a detailed definition and description of the following:

1. The aims and objectives in terms of contribution to the programme as a whole.
2. Its relationship to other modules.
3. Functions, activities and transactions in terms of intellectual and physical control and exploitation of records.
4. Performance measurement criteria, both quantitative and qualitative.
5. 'Critical success factors'.
6. Responsibility for management and operation.
7. Responsibility for resourcing in terms of personnel, money, supporting services, etc.
8. Production of operating procedures and standards, including documentation, for example forms, report formats, procedural manual.

The design must take into account all relevant constraints, both fixed and variable, as defined in the programme specification.

The processes and techniques, as well as the pace, of design vary for each module, and for systems within modules, depending on these factors, on the nature of the module itself and on the extent to which it is intended to be technology-dependent in the widest sense. A wide range of techniques can be used to produce and present designs, drawing on similar sources to those available for analysis and specification. Again, it is important to make the designs for each module meaningful to all departmental staff who are affected by it, maintaining the balance between technicality and simplicity. Diagrammatic and pictorial representations of systems and features should be used wherever possible to supplement detailed textual descriptions. If the design is technology-dependent, samples should be acquired (for furniture, stationery, etc.) or demonstrations arranged.

A work plan of draft–test–confirm–finalise needs to involve departmental staff at a number of levels and in a variety of ways, either individually or in groups, depending on the planned impact of each module. For example, if classification of records is intended to operate at departmental level, many more staff need to be involved in the testing and approval of systems than if it is intended to operate at a lower level. The design of a micrographics system requires the involvement of the departmental staff responsible for the records to be included in the system, the legal and audit personnel responsible for monitoring 'corporate' interests, and the specialist micrographics staff responsible for the operation of such systems, to ensure that the proposed system is acceptable to all parties. It may be necessary or appropriate to vary the pace of work on different modules to obtain maximum benefit from the necessary 'user participation', although it is important to maintain a relative balance of progress as far as possible, in order to minimise unnecessary 'double-handling', and retrospective reconciliation in ensuring appropriate integration of the individual modules.

As with the original specification, the production and presentation of designs should take account of any house style. It is likely that several draft designs will be produced for discussion, amendment and informal approval at various levels before the final versions can be presented for formal authorisation at the appropriate level. Formal authorisation in writing for the design of each programme module is essential and must be obtained at a level which can commit the organisation to the provision of the necessary resourcing for implementation. Implementation should not begin prior to this being obtained, unless specific internal circumstances dictate otherwise.

Phase IV: Implementation

The objectives of this phase are to establish each module of the programme to fully operational status and to train departmental staff in the operation of the programme.

Implementation can be carried out either as a single, continuous exercise or as a series of progressive steps, phasing the introduction of elements within modules and of modules within the programme as a whole. The most appropriate approach is determined by business imperatives and priorities, the timescale involved and available, the nature of existing systems and the availability of the required resources. Establishment of individual modules involves disposal of redundant records from existing systems and may entail setting up completely new systems from scratch and/or converting existing systems, wholly or in part. In either case it may be necessary to operate parallel systems for an interim period, to facilitate completion of outstanding matters from existing systems or the training of staff, or to minimise the disruption of a complex or time-consuming implementation process.

The training requirements of individual departmental staff are determined by their role and status in the organisation and in relation to the programme and by the relative newness of the programme modules with which they will be concerned. A 'common denominator' level of knowledge about the principles and operation of the programme is required by everyone. For staff with specific responsibility for management and operation of the programme, those in managerial and professional roles require detailed knowledge of both methodologies and procedures, while those in administrative, clerical and secretarial roles need detailed knowledge only of procedures. Other staff require sufficiently detailed knowledge of procedures to enable them to comply with the operation of the system as users, and their requirements may vary according to their status. Managerial and professional personnel may have contact with the programme only through secretaries or assistants, whereas others are likely to have more direct contact through the nature of their work.

A variety of techniques can be used to provide the required training. The relative merits of direct techniques (for example meetings, seminars, workshops) and indirect techniques (for example manuals, posters, audio-visual presentations) should be assessed in relation to the numbers of staff involved, their roles and status in the organisation, the level of detail required and the available timescale. Indirect methods are excellent for communication of general information and can have a strong impact, particularly through careful use of humour and visual presentation. Where a greater level of detail is necessary, direct methods which allow questions to be asked and answered are generally more effective. In selecting the most appropriate techniques, and in carrying out training, it is advisable to draw on any available in-house training expertise and to make full use of established internal training or communication structures. For example, a regular cycle of staff meetings provides a ready-made framework for presentation of a standard audio-visual training package.

The establishment of the programme modules and the training of departmental staff should take place simultaneously, as far as possible, to enable the new systems to be operated fully and effectively from 'day one', with appropriate support and assistance from project staff. Consideration should be given to setting up interim 'help-desk' facilities where project staff can be contacted to deal with problems or queries about the programme arising from implementation and initial operation.

Post-implementation

A comprehensive review of the programme should be carried out within six to twelve months of 'day one' in order to evaluate its effectiveness in terms of the aims, objectives and cost-benefit projections detailed in the strategic business plan and, if necessary or appropriate, to amend it to improve its effectiveness. The review should be carried out on the basis of the performance measurement criteria defined for each system as part of its design and should consist of physical inspection of systems and discussion with selected departmental staff from all areas involved, followed by analysis of the results, and design and implementation of any required amendments. If possible, the review should be conducted by the original project staff, because they are the most familiar with the systems involved.

The use of a standard form to set out the relevant performance measurement criteria for each module and to record the results of the review against these criteria will provide a specific focus for the review processes. All systems should be physically inspected and the results recorded. The selection of departmental staff to participate in the review should reflect a range of experience of the programme, including both users and those responsible for its management and operation. The discussion with staff can be conducted individually or in groups, where useful feedback can be obtained from an interchange of ideas. Following the collection and collation of the review data, analysis and any necessary design work should be carried out by repeating the relevant processes from Phases II and III, comparing the results of the review against the programme modules as implemented. Implementation of necessary amendments should take place as soon as possible after the review.

The programme manager should produce a formal report on the results of the review, detailing any amendments made to the programme as originally implemented and revising the aims, objectives and cost–benefit projections if appropriate. This report, or selected information from it, should be disseminated through similar channels to those used for the original strategic business plan, to maintain awareness of the programme and its purpose at all levels of the organisation.

The completion of the post-implementation review is the final stage in the initial development of the programme and should be the first stage in its mature development life-cycle of operate–review–amend–operate. A planned schedule of such reviews is essential to ensure that the programme maintains and justifies its position within the organisation by growing and changing with it to remain relevant and responsive to business needs.

CHAPTER 4

ESTABLISHING RETENTION CONTROL

ELIZABETH A. PARKER & PETER EMMERSON

CONCERN over the retention of records and its associated problems is often a major factor in the initial development of a records management programme. Although, as has been suggested in previous chapters, there are other important considerations, it is essential to deal with this element of records management intelligently, comprehensively, and systematically.

The overall aim of a retention module within a records management programme is to ensure that records are retained for as long as they have positive value for an organisation and for no longer, and that they are controlled efficiently and effectively during that time. Records have 'positive value' when they are required for the conduct of an organisation's business in terms of operations and compliance with regulatory and legal requirements. They are controlled efficiently and effectively when they are retained in a manner appropriate to the nature and level of their activity.

The specific objectives of a retention module are therefore:

(a) to determine the value of records in relation to operational, regulatory and legal requirements;
(b) to define retention periods for records under each of these categories of requirements;
(c) to define the life-cycle of records within their maximum retention periods; and
(d) to operate an administrative framework which ensures that records are retained in the most appropriate manner for the defined periods and are disposed of promptly thereafter.

In addition to these, an organisation may wish to retain certain records as archives for historical or research purposes, or in relation to a specific business objective, for example, publicity.

Operational requirements

Assessment of operational requirements for the retention of records must be based initially on an analysis of the relative 'internal' importance of business functions, activities and transactions. This analysis seeks to answer the following questions:

1. Which functions, activities and transactions form the 'core' of the business? What does the organisation primarily exist to do?
2. Which functions, activities and transactions are 'vital' to the business? In the event of a disaster, which of these must continue in order to maintain the viability of the organisation in business and to protect the rights of the organisation, its shareholders, employees, creditors and the public?
3. Which functions, activities and transactions are neither 'core' nor 'vital' to the business? Which are 'nice to have' rather than essential and which only exist to support the 'core' of the business?

Records which relate to 'core' or 'vital' functions, activities or transactions are likely to be of greater overall value to an organisation than records which do not. However, for any business function, activity or transaction, operations will be carried out at a number of organisational levels, becoming less 'important' as the work flows downwards, from the general to the specific and from the varied to the routine.

Second, assessment should be based on an analysis of the relative 'external' importance of business functions, activities and transactions:

1. Which functions, activities and transactions are unique to the organisation?
2. Which are common to all organisations operating in the same business area?
3. What is the nature of the external business environment of the organisation? Is that environment subject to trade or other regulations? Does the organisation have a defined market and is it in competition for a share of that market?

Records which relate to aspects of the scope, substance or operation of the business and which are unique to an organisation are likely to be of greater value than records which do not. Assessment of value should take into account the way in which other organisations in the same business value their records. This is particularly important for organisations operating in a competitive business environment, where there may be advantage to be gained by retaining or disposing of particular records, and where appropriate, building this into a marketing strategy. For example, in a business which is customer-driven, such as banking, an organisation may see competitive advantage in retaining particular records in order to protect the rights of its customers, and by advertising this approach to its existing and potential customer base.

Professional or trade associations or other bodies, such as the British Standards Institution, may produce guidelines, codes of practice, standards or regulations on any aspect of a 'business' to which they relate, either on their own initiative, or in response to demand from member organisations or to clarify specific legislation, and these may have implications for retention of records. It is essential to establish the nature of the authority of such bodies. An organisation may be able to operate only through membership of such a body and by compliance with its requirements. Alternatively, membership and compliance may be voluntary or discretionary but advisable for organisations operating in a competitive business environment.

A third factor in assessment is an analysis of the role of records in the operation of business functions, activities and transactions:

1. Are records created and used as an integral part of operations? Is their value 'evidential'?
2. Are records used to enable or facilitate operations of which they do not form an integral part? Is their value 'informational'?
3. In either case, do records have continuing value following completion of the operations to which they relate?

The relative merits of 'evidential' and 'informational' value must be assessed in the specific context in which the records occur. Records occurring at a low level in relation to core functions may have high evidential value but low informational value, whereas the opposite may apply to records generated at a high level in relation to non-vital functions. Records may have on-going value, either informational or evidential, following the completion of the operation to which they relate. Records which are likely to have on-going value to an organisation are those that relate to: organisational structure; management of business; development of operational policy, methodology and procedure; establishment of precedent; and developmental work, when retention may avoid the need for future 're-invention of the wheel'. Records which are unlikely to have on-going value are those that deal with routine application and implementation of established policy or precedent.

Audit requirements

Assessment of requirements to retain records, for the purposes of regulation and control in order to protect the rights of an organisation and, as appropriate, its shareholders, employees, creditors and the general public, must take into account the requirements of both internal and external authorities.

Internal inspection, control or auditing authorities

These are concerned with the functional efficacy of internal control systems, and may be involved in advisory, executive, reporting or testing activities in relation to such control systems in any area of the business at any level. It is essential to establish their objectives and scope and the nature of their authority, as implementation of their 'requirements' may be either mandatory or discretionary.

External auditors or auditing authorities

These are employed by an organisation for either 'private' or 'statutory' purposes. A private audit is one undertaken at the request of an organisation even though there is no legal obligation for an audit to be conducted. The scope of such an audit is defined by the organisation concerned and, although this will generally involve business functions, activities and transactions which relate to the management of finance and accounts, specialised assignments may involve other business areas. Compliance with requirements of external auditors arising from private audits is at the discretion of the organisation. A statutory audit is undertaken in compliance with the Companies Act, which requires the accounts of every limited company, both public and private, to be audited annually by a professionally qualified auditor. The scope of this audit is largely determined by the legislation, which the organisation and the auditors have no authority to vary in any way. Compliance with 'requirements' leading to or arising from this process is therefore mandatory.

The various auditing authorities may define retention periods for specific series of records in relation to specific functions, activities or transactions. Alternatively, they may only define a period within which audit or inspection will take place or during which compliance is required in relation to a particular area of the business, leaving considerable room for interpretation as to which specific series of records will be involved.

In general, retention requirements in this category involve

records of evidential value from the establishment of policy through to its implementation – the prime records of any business function, activity or transaction. In the absence of specific guidance from the appropriate authorities, it is advisable to retain all such records for the maximum period within which audit or inspection may take place, or for which compliance is required.

Legal requirements

Assessment of legal requirements to retain records for the purposes of protecting the rights and monitoring the obligations of the organisation, its shareholders and employees and the general public must take into account both statutory and other legislative requirements and those which may be inferred from common law. In the case of legislative requirements, a distinction should be made between those which are mandatory and those which may be interpreted as discretionary.

Legislation, in the form of statute, statutory instrument, Rule or Order, Order in Council or by-law, may specifically require those to whom its provisions apply to 'maintain' records (in some cases of specific content or format) in relation to the circumstances to which its provisions apply and for the period during which they apply. These provisions may include specific penalties for non-compliance. This category includes the following widely applicable statutes:

Companies Acts;
VAT Act 1983;
Factories Act 1961; and
Disabled Persons (Employment) Act 1944.

Alternatively, legislation may be specific only in terms of the circumstances to which its provisions apply and the period for which they apply, leaving considerable scope for discretion in creating, maintaining and retaining records in relation to those circumstances. This category includes:

Limitation Act 1980;
Finance Acts;
Taxes Management Act 1970;
Employment Protection Act 1975 and the Employment Protec-
    tion (Consolidation) Act 1978;
Sex Discrimination Act 1975;
Race Relations Act 1976;
Rehabilitation of Offenders Act 1974;
Fatal Accidents Act 1976; and
Data Protection Act 1984.

Legislation may apply to an organisation for the following reasons:

1. The fact of its existence as a legal entity; e.g. Limitation Act
    1980, Finance Acts, Taxes Management Act 1970, Employ-
    ment Protection Act 1975, Sex Discrimination Act 1975, Race
    Relations Act 1976, Rehabilitation of Offenders Act 1974, Fatal
    Accidents Act 1976, Disabled Persons (Employment) Act 1944.
2. The fact and nature of its existence as a legal entity; e.g.
    Companies Acts, Partnership Act 1890, Trade Union and
    Labour Relations Act 1974, Local Government Acts.
3. The nature of its business; e.g. Consumer Protection Act 1987,
    Latent Damage Act 1986, VAT Act 1983, Factories Act 1961,
    Road Traffic Act 1972, Licensing Act 1964, Design Copyright
    Act 1968, Financial Services Act 1987.

The legislation may apply automatically as a prerequisite or result
of the existence and conduct of business by the organisation, or may
be dependent on an occurrence of the circumstances to which the
provisions of the legislation apply. It is therefore essential to
establish the legal status of the organisation as, for example, a
company (private or public), partnership, charity, university, local
government authority or statutory body, and also the nature of its
business.

It is also essential to ensure that all supplementary provisions to
any particular piece of legislation are taken into account. For
example, Schedule 7 of the VAT Act 1983 lays down general
requirements for record-keeping. More detailed requirements are
contained in the VAT (General) Regulations 1985 (Amendment)
Regulations and in Customs and Excise Notice No. 700, which gave
effect to a change in the retention period for VAT-related
documentation from three to six years, promulgated as a clause in
the Finance Act 1985.

Legal requirements for retention involve records of evidential
value which form the prime integral documentation of any business
function. Where applicable legislation specifically requires maintenance or retention of records, it is advisable to comply with these
requirements. Where maintenance alone is required, the record
should then be retained for the period for which the provisions of
the legislation apply. An organisation may choose non-compliance
with such legislation as a positive 'risk-management' decision,
taking into account both the likelihood of discovery of non-
compliance by the relevant enforcing authorities and the nature of
the penalties which would be incurred in such an event and
balancing them against the cost of retaining the records.

Where legislation does not specifically require maintenance or retention of records, an organisation should assess the risk of falling foul of the legislation in the course of its operations, the records which are likely to be required in the event of such an occurrence, the period for which the provisions of the legislation apply and the cost of retaining the relevant records for that period in order to reach a decision on the relative cost–benefit of retention. For example, the maintenance and retention of a full set of prime documentation relating to routine contracts may be too labour-intensive and costly for an organisation to justify as insurance against an occasional occurrence of legal action for breach of contract. The organisation could therefore decide to dispose of this documentation within the period prescribed by the relevant provision of the Limitation Act 1980 when it ceases to have operational value and accept that, in the event of any legal action arising, it would be unable to provide an adequate defence and would incur a loss as a result.

The Limitation Act 1980

It is appropriate to examine the provisions of this Act more closely because it has been, and remains, a major influence on the retention policies of many organisations in the United Kingdom and is frequently quoted as the authority for retaining large quantities of records for long periods. Specifically, the Act lays down time limits following which the courts will not accept actions in respect of, for example, breach of contract, recovery of debt or damages for personal injury. For obligations under simple contract the period is limited to six years from the last date at which any action in the matter took place. The limitation period for contracts under seal is twelve years. Actions for personal injury are barred after three years from the cause of action, with the proviso that the period should begin to run from the time at which the individual could reasonably have been expected to be aware of the injury. This provision allows for the problems arising from residual injury or disease which only manifests itself some years after the specific cause.

The Act makes no specific mention of a need to retain records in defence of such actions. The need to do so is, therefore, more a matter of prudence than of compulsion or obligation. Once again it is a question of risk management. If the organisation is sure of its business procedures and controls, then the risk of non-retention can clearly be assessed and a realistic approach adopted. The provisions of specific statutes, for example the Companies Act on accounting records, and the VAT Act (as amended), may well provide an overriding requirement. However, for organisations not subject to such statutes a more flexible and discretionary assessment of their responsibilities is possible. In all such cases, it may be possible to rely on information in a more summarised form and at a higher level in the documentary chain, rather than being forced to retain the bulky prime documentation. In addition, most organisations are aware, at a fairly early stage, of those contracts and relationships which are likely to cause problems and, consequently, can ensure the retention of the directly related records.

Naturally, in the case of personal injury, the period during which the possibility of an action remains may be quite extensive. It might be prudent, in appropriate circumstances, to retain, for example, summary records of accidents or exposure to hazardous conditions throughout the working lives of individuals as a means of verifying claims or providing defence. On the other hand the business may be prepared to accept the risk of not being in a position to refute claims and, consequently, to dispose of the records concerned.

Requirements to 'create', 'maintain' or 'retain' records may be expressly stated or implied by, or inferred from, common-law sources, such as case-law. There is no direct obligation to take account of such sources, and a similar form of risk-assessment to that described above should be applied.

European Community influences

An additional dimension has been added to the legislative and regulatory framework in the United Kingdom by the gradual application and extension of European Community law and regulation to this country. This has occurred both as a result of the Community Directives which seek to harmonise laws in the member countries (for example, Data Protection, Product Liability) and as a result of the regulatory requirements of the treaties establishing the Community in general (Treaty of Rome) and those affecting specific industries (for example, Treaty of Paris establishing the European Coal and Steel Community). The requirements of competition and fair-pricing policies promulgated by the EEC have in some cases made the retention of, for example, primary accounting and sales documentation, more onerous than national legislation or regulation. The potential fines for failing to produce information requested by the Commission's inspectors are considerably higher than those likely to be imposed under national law and could substantially change the balance of risk in any calculation. The Commission Inspectorate also has very extensive powers in calling for, and obtaining, the records containing such information.

This influence is likely to become even greater with the introduction of the single European Market in 1992 and organisations now involved, or proposing to become involved, in European activities should be aware of the provisions which apply to them. The key in this area, as in any other, is to be aware of the regulatory framework within which the business or organisation functions and to draw on the expertise of specialist legal and commercial advisers to establish the maximum requirements which are thereby imposed. It should then be possible to make a more reasoned value judgement of the risks involved in not retaining records. It cannot be stressed too strongly that this needs to be done within an established corporate policy and a managed programme rather than leaving it to the *ad hoc* development of local initiatives.

Determining archival value

The determination of archival value is much more difficult than defining the retention period of documents for normal business purposes. Appraisal of this kind remains one of the major skills of the professional archivist, and those organisations that do not have the benefit of in-house expertise and that wish to ensure the survival of records as a permanent archive holding should at least seek expert advice. The pressures faced, particularly in a business environment, are twofold. The first comes from the employer to retain as little as possible, and the second comes from the potential researcher to provide as wide a range of materials as possible to feed research interests. This may be a very difficult balance to maintain and must necessarily lean towards the needs and wishes of the creators of the records.

The judgement is essentially subjective but can be built around a series of criteria which stress the use to which the records might be put within the creating organisation and which, by and large, will serve all other users of the records reasonably well. The application of techniques similar to those that have been described earlier in this chapter to meet the more immediate needs of the records management programme will provide the right kind of framework for this more esoteric appraisal. There are a number of values to be assessed and once again they are broadly evidential and informational.

Evidential value

Essentially, the person carrying out the appraisal is seeking to build up a picture of what the organisation did, why it did it, how and where it carried out its business, whom it employed to do it and finally, what the results of that activity were. A number of questions arise:

- What indication do the records give of the operation of the creating organisation and its business?
- How was the organisation structured and what did it do?
- What were its substantive functions and activities?

Records which aid in the reconstruction of past activity may be of use in future planning or, at least, in using the past activities of the business to help market those of the present. In broad terms, records which have this type of value are those which show the origins of the organisation as a whole or its constituent parts, why it came into being and the processes which led to its establishment. In addition records which demonstrate how the business or department was organised or structured to carry out its tasks and any changes to that structure and organisation which took place will also be valuable.

There is a need to demonstrate the role of each component part or unit of the organisation: what it was responsible for; how it achieved its objectives; and how it fitted operationally into the overall business. Particularly important are those records which demonstrate how policies were arrived at and decisions taken at each level within the organisation and which illustrate the transmission of those policies and decisions to the remainder of the organisation. The minutes and papers of the board of directors of a company, for example, as well as those of senior executive committees or bodies, would automatically fall within this category. This example demonstrates that many of the records which fall within these categories have a high, and long-term, operational value which is a guide to their ultimate value for retrospective research. The reverse does not apply, however, and records with low operational value and use in the first part of their life-cycle may still have long-term value in the future. In this, as in other areas of records analysis, frequency of use can only really be used as a negative indicator, confirming the status of records already designated as being of little value.

Other records which may provide valuable data on the creating organisation are those which deal with procedures and operational methods and those showing the internal development of policy and strategy and the arguments put forward in support of that policy. These, along with the records of research and development into new products, processes, methodologies and markets may prove particularly useful to the creating organisation, too, as it seeks to plan for the future. Records which relate to people, either customers or employees, as individuals are of course very sensitive, but those providing aggregated personal data are invaluable for personnel planning and in the development of, for example, improved medical facilities and services and occupational health schemes.

One final area of interest would be in those records which reflect the external involvement of the organisation with, for example, central and local government, regulatory bodies, trade associations, trade unions and international bodies and of the influence of those contacts on the development of policy. All of these help to build up a picture of the context in which the organisation's main functions, activities and transactions are carried out.

Informational value

Through the preservation of essentially organisation-centred material, a good deal of incidental information will survive relating to that organisation in its wider context and relationships. Data arising from and used by the organisation in its day-to-day operations may be equally valuable for retrospective research in another field. It is a fact of archival life that surviving records are frequently used for purposes which would not have been imagined by their creators. Additionally, many organisations collect special external data in the course of their own business which may subsequently form the raw material of additional studies both inside and outside the structure. Market research survey data, for example, may well provide useful demographic or social insights which were not in the minds of those carrying out the original research. However, in the context of a records management programme, any attempt to 'second guess' and anticipate research trends should always be subordinate to the provision of usable and worthwhile information to serve the business needs and purposes of the creating organisation.

Development of a retention module

The development of a retention module involves the identification and collection of data on records series, the analysis of individual series to assess their value, the definition of retention periods, and a retention life-cycle for each series.

The process for collection of data on records series is described in the previous chapter. Following completion of this process, each series should be analysed in terms of its purpose and content in relation to business functions, activities and transactions and in terms of its relationship to other series, in order to assess its value to the organisation in meeting operational, regulatory and legal requirements and to define a retention period in each applicable category of requirements. Assessment of value and definition of retention periods should be undertaken independently for each category, to facilitate identification and incorporation of subsequent amendments in any one category, for example due to legislative changes. If possible, assessment of archival value should also be made at this stage.

For series which are 'constant' in terms of their generic content (for example, invoices, minutes, case files), it should be assumed that their value will also be constant. Their defined retention periods will, therefore, be applied repetitively and the records destroyed at the end of that period unless there is a specific reason not to do so at that time (for example, active litigation involving the records) or unless they have been selected for permanent preservation as archives. However, for series which are 'variable' in terms of their generic content (such as 'subject' files) the allocation of specific retention periods for repetitive application in this way is inappropriate. Within these series, files need to be appraised individually to establish their value. By their very nature, such files may well contain a mixture of substantive and policy material and routine documentation. It cannot be assumed that files with the same title contain records of equal value and, therefore, that a retention decision relating to one can be applied safely to another. Such series should be highlighted to ensure that their contents are reviewed on a piece-by-piece basis at the end of the defined retention period for the series as a whole. Any records of continuing value can then be identified and appropriate action taken, including selection as archives.

With limited exceptions, retention periods must consist of two elements:

(a) a starting-point or 'trigger', because the conditions which affect retention vary; and
(b) a period of time.

The use of a code (Fig. 4.1) to identify the range of applicable starting points simplifies administrative effort.

A unique reference number should be applied to each records series identified and a standard format (Fig. 4.2) used to document the assessment of value and the definition of retention periods for each series. This ensures consistency and assists in the process of reconciliation across the organisation. A records series may occur in

Retention code		
CW	—	Current week
CM	—	Current month
CQ	—	Current quarter
CY	—	Current year
K	—	Creation
ACT	—	Active, i.e. as long as required for active operations (unpredictable)
AUD	—	Completion of audit
P	—	Permanent
S	—	Settlement, e.g. of legal action (specified)
T	—	Termination, e.g. of employment or contract (specified)
+	Required period of time in weeks/months/years	

Fig. 4.1: Retention code.

relation to more than one function, activity or transaction and a single function, activity or transaction may be carried out by more than one area of the organisation.

RECORDS APPRAISAL

DEPARTMENT	SECTION	UNIT
TITLE		REF.

OPERATIONAL	AUDIT	LEGAL
ASSESSMENT	ASSESSMENT	ASSESSMENT

RETENTION	ACTION	RETENTION	ACTION	RETENTION	ACTION

ARCHIVAL ASSESSMENT	NOTES

Fig. 4.2: Records appraisal form.

When analysis, assessment of value and definition of retention periods are complete, confirmation of assessments and authorisation of the defined retention periods for each category of requirements must be obtained from appropriate departmental staff.

It is essential that confirmation of assessments is obtained from qualified staff. Assessments of value in relation to operational requirements must be validated by those in a position to assess evidential *and* informational value in both the short *and* the long term, and assessments of value in terms of audit and legal requirements by professionals in these fields. In most organisations, it is unlikely that any one person has the necessary expertise or experience to confirm all assessments of value and defined retention periods for any category of requirements, particularly where a business function, activity or transaction involves more than one organisational area. A sequence of confirmations is therefore likely to be required for each records series involving staff in operational, audit and legal functions across the organisation and at a variety of levels. Confirmation of assessments should be indicated by signature of relevant documentation by all those involved.

It is equally essential that authorisation of retention periods is obtained from personnel of sufficiently senior status to provide impetus and support for the implementation of the module as well as to commit the organisation to any consequent cost, workload or legal liability. This is likely to mean a departmental manager or equivalent and it is, therefore, unlikely that those involved in confirmation of assessments are also of appropriate status to provide authorisation for retention periods. Regardless of the number of staff involved in the confirmation process, it is essential that one overall authorisation is obtained for retention periods in relation to each category of retention requirements. Again, authorisation should be indicated by signature of the relevant documentation by all those involved.

It is essential to collate the data required for the confirmation and authorisation processes in a standard format (Fig. 4.3). This can be combined with the format used for assessment of value and definition of retention periods, which will minimise administrative effort and avoid the impression of an endless chain of documentation. However, there are potential disadvantages to this approach, principally that too much incidental data is provided which is not actually required by the personnel involved. Consequently, the use of a separate specific format is preferable. The following is the minimum data required for each series:

RECORDS RETENTION AUTHORITY					EDITION PAGE OF
DEPARTMENT		SECTION		UNIT	

REF.	TITLE	P	RETENTION/ACTION			NOTES
			OPERATIONAL	AUDIT	LEGAL	

AUTHORISATION		
OPERATIONAL	AUDIT	LEGAL
POSITION	POSITION	POSITION
NAME	NAME	NAME
SIGNATURE	SIGNATURE	SIGNATURE

Fig. 4.3: Records retention authority form.

1. The title.
2. Whether its status is 'prime' or 'non-prime'.
3. The retention period by category of requirement, i.e.
   (a) organisational;
   (b) legal; or } with specific justification
   (c) audit
4. The action following expiry of retention period.

It is important to establish an administrative framework for the processes of confirmation and authorisation to ensure consistency and completeness and, depending on the size of the organisation and its structure and culture, it may be necessary, or convenient, to separate the processes. It must be determined in advance who is to be involved, bearing in mind that changes may be necessary in the course of the exercise. A 'top-down' approach is essential to ensure that managers determine the appropriate involvement of their staff.

Confirmation and authorisation can be obtained either in individual sessions with the appropriate staff, or through committees with formal terms of reference specially convened for the purpose. There are advantages and disadvantages to the 'records committee' approach. Membership can be controlled and manipulated to ensure the involvement of the right people at the right time, and cross-fertilisation of expertise can be of considerable value in discussion of assessments and retention periods. However, it can be difficult either to confine committee members to decision-making in their own areas of expertise, or to maintain their commitment to the necessity for positive decisions rather than reliance on other members to cover their requirements. It is therefore essential that, if a 'records committee' approach is adopted, an option to approach the membership on an independent basis is retained.

Retention schedules

When authorisation of retention periods has been obtained, the life-cycle of each series should be determined and documented in retention schedules for implementation. The life-cycle of a records series is determined by dividing its total retention period (i.e. the maximum period defined across all categories of requirements) into relative periods of *active life*, i.e. required for immediate working purposes; and *inactive life*, i.e. required to be retained beyond active life for other purposes. For series to which repetitive retention periods should not be applied, as described earlier, the life-cycle should still be determined at series level, designating the point at which individual files within the series should be retired from active use and at which the content should be reviewed for on-going value. Life-cycle periods should be defined in the same way as retention periods, by a starting-point or 'trigger' and a period of time. Decisions on life-cycle periods should be made by those involved with the day-to-day use of the records, and no formal authorisation of these decisions is necessary, unless specifically required by the organisation.

Records retention schedules may be either *general* or *specific* in nature. Specific retention schedules cover a defined organisational or business area and include all records series occurring within that area. The major advantage of specific retention schedules is that they are tailored to their area of coverage in terms of the way in which records series are titled and organised and therefore require the minimum of interpretation for effective application. General (Fig. 4.4) retention schedules include records regardless of the organisational or business area in which they occur. Their main purpose is to deal with records series which are common to all organisational or business areas, in order to avoid repetition on specific retention schedules for each area. The principal potential disadvantage of general retention schedules is that they require interpretation for application in any particular area because of their need to use records series titles which are meaningful to a wide audience and because the records series included may be organised differently by different areas according to their individual size, complexity or operating procedures. For example, sales invoices

C.1. SALES DOCUMENTS

Retention Period

C.1.1	Customer's Complaints	
	To comply with ECSC requirements	C + 5
	To comply with VAT requirements only	C + 6
	To comply with Companies Act 1976	C + 6

If filed with the customer's order they should be destroyed with the order at the normal time (See 1.2 below).

C1.2	Customer's Orders	
	To comply with ECSC requirements	T + 5
	To comply with VAT requirements only	T + 6
	To comply with Companies Act 1976	T + 6

In some cases there are special long-term obligations in the contract and the orders should be kept for longer periods, which should be determained as soon as possible.   T + 6R

C.1.3	Enquiries	One year maximum

C.1.4   Estimates and Quotations

To comply with ECSC requirements (this will   T + 5
normally allow sufficient time for any queries to
be raised and any comparisons made between
estimated and actual costs)
To comply with VAT requirements only   T + 6
To comply with the Companies Act, 1976   T + 6
In some cases the quotation has special, longer
term, significance as part of the contract and should
be kept for the same period as the contract with
which it is associated.

C.1.5   Export Credit Guarantee Department Documents

Should be retained for three yaers after the period
covered or until the transaction concerned is
completed and final payment received. For this
purpose, where a claim has been made the
transaction is not to be considered as completed
until the claim has been finally settled.   T + 3

C.1.6   Long Date Budget Tabulations

Figures for the current year and the previous year
only should be retained for comparison.   C + 1

C.1.7   Short Date Budgets: Most Recent Forecasts

One year from the month for which the forecast is
made.   One year

Fig. 4.4:   An example of a general retention schedule.

may be filed individually by invoice number in a sales accounts section and filed with correspondence by customer name in a credit control section. An entry for 'sales invoice' on a general retention schedule would therefore require interpretation for application to what are, in fact, two separate records series. The usefulness of general retention schedules therefore depends to some extent on the method of their creation. A general retention schedule drawn up prior to the development of any specific retention schedules is more difficult to interpret and apply than one compiled by extracting records series of general occurrence from specific retention schedules, as the general schedule may then include retention periods for each occurrence of a particular records series.

A decision on the relative merits of specific and general retention schedules for a particular organisation should take into account the size and complexity of the organisation. In small companies, for instance, general schedules may be more suitable because of the limited number of records series occurring and their relative simplicity. In large corporations, specific retention schedules for defined areas are generally more efficient and effective. It is worth considering a combination of the two types of schedules, whereby a general schedule is used for broad guidance and particular areas also have specific schedules tailored to their own operational procedures.

The content and format of both specific and general retention schedules is similar. They should contain at least the following data for each records series, arranged in a columnar format (Fig. 4.5).

RECORDS RETENTION SCHEDULE				EDTION PAGE OF		
DEPARTMENT		SECTION		UNIT		
REF.	TITLE	P	RETENTION/ ACTION			NOTES
			OFFICE	STORE	TOTAL	

Fig. 4.5: A records retention schedule.

(a) title;
(b) 'prime' or 'non-prime';
(c) active retention period;
(d) inactive retention period;
(e) total retention period; and
(f) action following expiry of total retention period.

Records series should be listed alphabetically by title either across the area of coverage of the schedule or within function, activity and transaction, although in some organisations and circumstances it may be more logical to compile schedules by form number, where individual forms constitute complete records series.

Additional data may be included depending on the overall objectives of the records management programme. For example, if there is a vital records protection module within the programme, it is necessary to indicate on the schedule which records series are designated as 'vital' to ensure that appropriate action is taken for their protection at each stage. Similarly, records series selected for preservation as archives, wholly or in part, should be highlighted. If security of information is a priority, it is useful to indicate the security classification of each records series to ensure that physical movement and ultimate disposal of records are effected in an appropriate manner.

When retention schedules are finalised, they must be distributed for implementation. The appropriate level of distribution will depend on the structure of the schedules and on the organisational culture. General retention schedules should obviously be distributed to all areas, while specific schedules need only be distributed to the area which they directly concern. Schedules may be given to all staff within each area or to designated individuals with local responsibility for compliance with their requirements.

Where the active life-cycle period of a records series is the same as its total retention period, the appropriate action in respect of records of that series can be taken at the end of that period. Where a series needs to be retained beyond its active life for other purposes, records of that series should be consigned to intermediate storage for their inactive life (see Chapter 5) with the appropriate action being taken at the end of the total retention period. This process ensures that records are retained in the most cost-efficient and effective manner for the periods required, that if necessary they are reviewed in a constructive and timely way and that they are promptly destroyed at the end of their useful life.

The major benefit of retention schedules is that they provide a framework for efficient and effective control of retention and disposal of records. This framework requires amendment as the organisational structure and business functions, activities and transactions change through natural evolution or in response to a catalyst such as change of ownership or introduction of new technology, with inevitable effects on the records produced. It is therefore essential to provide for review and revision of retention schedules at planned intervals, preferably annually, to add new records series, delete obsolete series and incorporate changes in retention requirements for on-going series. Additions of new records series and amendments to retention periods for existing series require repetition of the assessment, confirmation and authorisation processes. Deletions of records series should be authorised by the personnel responsible for their original inclusion.

Retention schedules which are not reviewed, and if necessary revised, on a regular basis are eventually more of a liability than an asset to the records management programme and to the organisation, as their content becomes at best irrelevant and at worst illegal.

CHAPTER 5

PROVIDING STORAGE FACILITIES

SHELLEY HARDCASTLE

Consultant, Britannia Data Management PLC

STORAGE is one of the main elements in the management of records (Fig. 5.1). It is also the area where the savings provided by a records management system are most immediate and recognisable.

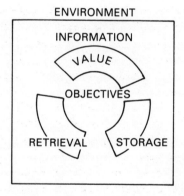

Fig. 5.1:   The main elements of records management.

Unfortunately managers focus on storage equipment and facilities without realising that the storage of records is a complex activity which involves the use of staff and of space, and needs to take into account factors such as security, ease and speed of access to records and environmental conditions.

As has already been shown a record can be seen as having a life-cycle. The three main stages in this cycle are current, non-current (or inactive) and archival. This assumes that a record has a use and a value. Redundancy of records is another key factor which needs to be considered when a records storage system is being designed. It makes little sense to tie up valuable resources keeping records which have little or no value. A system which is not purged of non-current material systematically and regularly impedes records retrieval. Any storage system should facilitate this purging process.

The primary costs of a storage system are accommodation and staff time. In an active records system, staff time devoted to putting away and retrieving records can account for up to 50 per cent of the cost. It makes sense therefore, to organise the storage in such a way as to make access and retrieval as rapid as possible.

In the non-current phase the amount of staff time spent handling records becomes less and the space costs more significant. It makes sense therefore to seek solutions which reduce the unit cost of storing records. At the non-current stage this can be done by using techniques similar to those used in warehousing. In such an arrangement retrieving a record is slower. However, an agreed delay on retrieval is acceptable provided it is known and allowances can then be made for it in the work schedule.

Records and office managers, therefore, need to take account of the activity or reference rate of records in their charge. Typically a record is most active in its first year. The rate normally drops to something like 20 per cent in the second year. After three years, less than 5 per cent are likely to be referenced. This is a generalised figure and the activity rate of specific record series should be monitored during the analytical programme described in Chapter 3. This is done to identify when records become redundant so that steps can be taken to remove them from costly office space.

Because the most significant cost migrates from staff to space as the activity rate declines, the objective changes accordingly. At the first stage while records are current and highly active, the staff costs are high. The objective, therefore, is to contain staff costs. At the second stage, when the records are non-current and reference is less frequent, the space cost is proportionately higher. The objective is therefore to make maximum use of the space available and reduce the space cost to the minimum.

An appreciation of these changing objectives is critical when designing a storage system for records. So too is a recognition that different methods of storage are appropriate at the different activity stages (Fig. 5.2).

Current records

Storage costs

Very few organisations know what it is costing them to store current records. While many know about the capital cost of storage

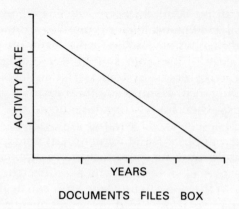

Fig. 5.2: Storage methods at different activity stages.

equipment, this information is of limited use. At a very basic level, it is important to know the equipment and space of storing a linear foot (35 centimetres) of records in a given floor area. For example, a two-drawer vertical filing cabinet takes up about 10 square feet (or 1 square metre) of usable floor space but only holds 4 linear feet (1.2 metres) of files. The top of the cabinet may provide a very useful surface for mugs and plants but the ratio of storage space to floor space is poor. The annual cost of storing records in a two-drawer filing cabinet in office space which costs £12 per square foot per annum is £120, i.e. £30 per linear foot or £60 per file drawer:

$$\frac{\text{annual cost/ft}^2 \times \text{ft}^2 \text{ occupied}}{\text{cabinet capacity}} = \text{unit cost of storage}$$

$$\frac{12 \times 10}{4} = 30$$

Even the use of larger, more cost-effective cabinets does not improve matters. One major government department discovered, when it carried out a records survey, that 10 per cent of its four-drawer filing cabinets were being under-utilised. The bottom drawer of the cabinets was often used for storing kettles, shoes and other miscellaneous material unrelated to records.

Staff costs

Though space costs are significant, staff costs are greater and therefore of greater importance. It has been estimated that clerical staff can spend more than 20 per cent of their time putting away or retrieving information. Much of this time is taken up with record handling. Executive staff also file and retrieve records. In 1989 a clerical post in London costing an employer £12,000 per annum could well have £2,400 of its cost allocated to record keeping. In an organisation which employs 30,000 staff, two thirds of whom are clerical/secretarial staff, the annual cost is likely to be in the region of £50 million (i.e. 20,000 staff × £2,400).

It is not difficult for a manager to estimate the cost of staff, space, equipment and supplies involved in managing records. This provides a useful benchmark. A perceptive manager will see the benefits to be gained in reducing the capital and running costs of records storage systems by the application of efficiency techniques.

Equipment

It is unwise to wait until space runs out before addressing the issue of storage. One opportunity which should certainly not be missed is when an organisation is relocating. This is an ideal time to look at the record-keeping systems because the space and equipment savings are quickly realisable. Strangely, the last thing to be thought about is the type of equipment to be used. This may be why some office planners do not produce effective, efficient systems. There has been an increasing trend towards selecting office equipment for its visual appearance. This interest in style seems to be all-pervasive in new office developments.

In certain circumstances the question of style is of paramount importance and may override considerations of cost-effectiveness, for example, in the front office of an advertising agency or in the chief executive's office. Generally, the aim should be to use storage equipment which is most suited to the needs of the users and is most space efficient. Such equipment need not be starkly utilitarian in appearance. Given that capital equipment costs are likely to be marginal to the system's costs as a whole, it should be possible to combine value for money with a stylish appearance.

The objective should be to select the most cost-effective system appropriate to the user's needs. This may not be the cheapest equipment available and ideally should be determined by the relative importance of the various factors – volume, usage, space and security – in a given situation. If, for example, there are less than 8 linear feet (2.4 metres) of records to be housed a four-drawer cabinet would be sufficient. When the volume of records exceeds the capacity of three four-drawer cabinets, shelf filing is more appropriate as it saves space and handling time. Mobile filing systems should be considered when a significant volume of records needs to be held close to the user and space is at a premium but relatively low retrieval rates are acceptable. 'Power filing' may be cost-justified for a large collection of records with a high retrieval rate. Use of colour coding can reduce handling costs significantly.

Additional factors also have to be considered such as budget constraints, maintenance costs, availability and cost of supplies and floor loading specifications. The quality of equipment and the discounts available also have an impact on price.

It is sensible to obtain details of equipment from a number of suppliers and to calculate the cost of storing a given volume of records for each type of equipment taking into account all cost elements – space occupied, handling time, maintenance and supplies, as well as the equipment itself.

Function, form, size and volume

The functional characteristics of records (what they are used for) and their physical characteristics (size and durability) are major factors to be assessed when choosing storage equipment. Function helps to determine how long records remain current and also the type of equipment most appropriate to house them.

Size and volume of records also have an impact. Records which are non-standard sizes, for example, computer print-out or bulky files, may require special adaptations to filing equipment. It can be difficult to find office space to keep large collections of records close to users.

Function

Most managers have a set of records which give them the policy framework within which they must operate. Such policy records may be small in volume in relation to the total records population. However, since these are the records which establish the principles by which the organisation operates, there is usually a need to keep them close to those users who will be expected to provide policy guidance and monitor activities against policy.

The storage system chosen will need to provide for extra security. If a manager has sole use of the records and the volume is small, they can be located in a four-drawer vertical cabinet. If the volume of records exceeds 24 linear feet (7 metres) or three four-drawer cabinets, then lockable lateral shelf filing cabinets may be more appropriate. Shared simultaneous access will be impeded by vertical filing.

More general operational records need a lower level of security. These can include anything from implementation of policy through to routine matters relating to hospitality, arrangements for visits, booking conference rooms and making travel arrangements. More ephemera is found in this area. Four-drawer filing cabinets will be appropriate for small volumes, but open lateral filing is more space-efficient for larger holdings.

Many managers accumulate background or reference material ranging from photocopies of published articles to trade literature and personnel instruction manuals. It may be small in volume, for example, personnel manuals, or it may be large in volume, for example, trade literature in an engineering company. The most appropriate type of storage may be library-style shelves.

Transactions

Transaction (or case) records are those which relate to a specific action, event, person or project. They form the bulk of any organisation's records, as much as 90 per cent in some instances.

Those transaction records which are needed to execute a specific function tend to have a relatively short life. For example, invoices normally have an active life of only weeks or months. Once the transaction has taken place and the audit has been carried out, the records will exist primarily only to satisfy legal or statutory requirements.

Project records and personnel files on the other hand may have a relatively long life – the design of a new aircraft or the duration of employment. Care should be taken to avoid such files becoming too bulky.

A key feature of these records is their potential to form large accumulations. Common problems experienced with such large series are misfiling, excessive retention of redundant records and slow retrieval times. The choice of storage systems is particularly critical. Drawer filing becomes less practical for case records and lateral filing more obviously beneficial because of the increased storage capacity. It may even be appropriate to look to rotary, mobile or 'power' filing to achieve maximum storage density (see pp. 71, 73 and 74).

Types of equipment

Vertical filing (drawer cabinets)

Vertical filing cabinets are available with two, three, four or five drawers which pull out and provide space for drop filing (Fig. 5.3 shows a two-drawer and a four-drawer cabinet). Files, folders or papers are viewed from above and are usually arranged from front to back of the drawers. Files can be placed loose in the drawers or supported in suspended pockets, to which visible guides or title strips may be attached. The drawers can usually be locked to provide some security. If the records to be stored are highly confidential, a security bar with a combination lock or padlock may be placed vertically across the front of the drawers. Modern vertical filing cabinets normally include an anti-tilt device, as a safety measure, which prevents more than one drawer being pulled open at any one time.

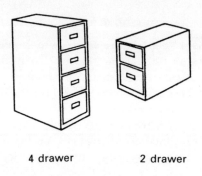

4 drawer   2 drawer

Fig. 5.3:   Vertical filing cabinets.

Users of vertical filing equipment commonly complain that its storage capacity is insufficient. Use of suspended pockets may reduce the storage capacity of a drawer by up to 25 per cent. Other common faults include suspended pockets splitting or slipping off the guide rails. Files may fall between pockets and may be overlooked when hidden beneath other files. Even with metal dividers files tend not to stay upright. The back of the drawers are less accessible than the front and files may fall flat and be overlooked. A bottom drawer left open is a safety hazard. If the anti-tilt mechanism fails, a top-heavy cabinet may fall over. Comparison of storage densities of two, three, four and five drawer cabinets are shown in Table 5.1.

Vertical filing systems also include cabinets with a wider drawer (Fig. 5.4). The files, folders or papers are still viewed from the top but they are arranged across the drawer, from side to side, rather than front to back. In a four-drawer model, 12 linear feet (3.6 metres) can be stored in 15 square feet (4.5 square metres) of office space, giving a ratio of 1 linear foot to 1.25 square feet (0.3 metres to 0.4 square metres).

Table 5.1 Storage density of vertical filing systems

Number of drawers	Storage capacity	Floor space occupied by equipment	Ratio Linear storage capacity	to	floor space
	lin ft (metres)	ft² (m²)	lin ft (metres)		ft³ (m³)
2	4 (1.2)	9 (3)	1 (0.3)	:	2.25 (0.7)
3	6 (2)	9 (3)	1 (0.3)	:	1.5 (0.5)
4	8 (2.4)	9 (3)	1 (0.3)	:	1.1 (0.3)
5	10 (3)	9 (3)	1 (0.3)	:	0.9 (0.2)

Fig. 5.4: Vertical filing cabinet with wider drawers.

Lateral filing

Lateral or horizontal filing cabinets usually have between two and seven or sometimes eight shelves. The files or folders are viewed from the side and are arranged from side to side, normally left to right. Files can be placed:

(a) loose on the shelves with metal dividers;
(b) in suspended pockets; or
(c) in plastic open-ended boxes – visible guides or title strips can be added to the suspended pockets.

Colour-coded tabs may also be added to the folders on the shelves, in the boxes or to the suspended pockets.

Lateral cabinets are available with lockable fronts in various forms (see Fig. 5.5). The standard 6ft × 3ft (2 m × 1 m) steel cupboard has two vertical axis doors which can be locked. Some cabinets have pull-down blinds in a PVC material or pull-down flexible plastic or metal strip shutters. Other units have individual up-and-over, horizontal axis, garage-style, doors. Taller units may be stabilised against each other back-to-back or fixed to a wall. However, because there is little mechanical friction, stability is not generally a matter for concern. A platform or stool is necessary to allow staff access to the top shelves when taller units are used.

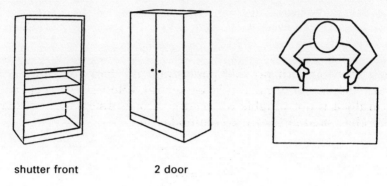

shutter front   2 door

Fig. 5.5:   Lateral cabinets.

Common complaints from users include the inaccessibility of the records stored on the higher shelves. Also suspended pockets split easily or slip off the guide rails causing files to fall out of the back. PVC blinds are not robust and easily tear or split. They act as dust covers rather than providing real security. Metal and plastic shutters are prone to jamming if used clumsily, making the records inaccessible for a period. Blind and shutter locks at the base of cabinets are not ideal and may be damaged by cleaning staff. They tend to jam easily as well as being less accessible. Comparison of storage densities of horizontal filing systems is shown in Table 5.2.

Table 5.2 Storage density of horizontal filing systems

Number of shelves	Storage capacity	Floor space occupied* by equipment	Ratio		
			Linear storage capacity	to	floor space
	lin ft (metres)	ft² (m²)	lin ft (metres)		ft² (m²)
2	6 (2)	12 (4)	1 (0.3)	:	2.5 (0.75)
3	9 (3)	12 (4)	1 (0.3)	:	1.3 (0.4)
4	12 (4)	12 (4)	1 (0.3)	:	1.1 (0.3)
5	15 (5)	12 (4)	1 (0.3)	:	0.8 (0.25)
6	18 (6)	12 (4)	1 (0.3)	:	0.6 (0.2)
7	21 (7)	12 (4)	1 (0.3)	:	0.5 (0.15)

*including access space

The benefits of using lateral equipment include higher storage density and faster access thereby reducing staff costs. Files are easier to identify and less effort is required to insert and remove them from the system. Typical storage/retrieval speeds range from thirty to forty items per hour whereas vertical filing is estimated at twenty-five to thirty items per hour. In addition lateral units allow for multiple access.

Racking/open shelving

Open shelving with no side panels and no doors or shutters is particularly economical for large record volumes (see Fig. 5.6). Naturally it is not suitable for secure records unless the racks are themselves sited in secure accommodation.

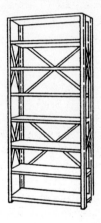

Fig. 5.6: Open shelving.

Suspended systems

It is worth looking at the suspended system which is used in both vertical and lateral systems as a separate concept (see Fig. 5.7). This system holds records in containers, either cardboard or plastic pockets, suspended from rails fitted into cabinets. These folders help to reduce misfiling and provide tidy storage but add to equipment costs, reduce storage space by as much as 25 per cent and are cumbersome to alter. Setting-up time and the creation of identifiers or guides needs to be taken into account. The records are identified by using tabs attached to the pockets which may come adrift and fall off. The advantage is that, provided the tabs remain on the pocket, it is evident that a file does exist, even though it may have been temporarily withdrawn for reference.

Fig. 5.7:　Suspended system.

Colour-coding

In conjunction with lateral units, the use of colour-coded files, folders and wallets can bring significant benefits in terms of both reduced staff costs and reduced misfiling. There is a common misconception that colour coding simply means buying a range of the five standard colours and the whole jacket has a colour. In modern colour-coded systems this concept is taken a stage further as the file reference, which can be either alphabetical or numerical, is itself colour-coded. For example, with the name Brown, the first three letters of the name appear in bold script in a coloured box. Each letter has a unique colour code so that if the file is misplaced the colour pattern is interrupted and the misfile is easily visible. In addition, file references are visible from a distance so that users can identify the target location from some distance away and thus reach the required file more rapidly. This significantly reduces staff time spent in putting away and retrieving material. Colour-coding is particularly suited to filing of individual cases and in North America studies have shown average savings in staff time of as much as 20 per cent.

Unit box filing

Colour-coding is often used in conjunction with lateral filing housed in plastic open-ended boxes 4, 5 or 6 inches wide (10, 12.5 15 centimetres), foolscap or A4 size.

The boxes are suspended on rails attached to a wall, or in a free-standing frame or mounted in cupboards (see Fig 5.8). The great advantage is that the system is easy to expand or rearrange and boxes can be inserted where needed. Free-standing systems are normally seven tiers high and can be arranged back-to-back giving very high storage densities, for example 2.3 linear feet in 1 square foot (2.1 metres per square metre).

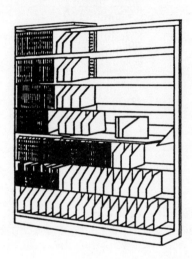

Fig. 5.8: Unit box filing system.

Rotary/carousel filing

Rotary equipment allows active records to be located adjacent to users giving simultaneous access to more than one user (see Fig. 5.9). Rotary systems are space-efficient, a five-tier system holding 30 linear feet (9 metres) of files in about 17 square feet (5 square metres) of floor space – 1.75 linear feet in 1 square foot (1.6 metres per square metre)

Records are stored on a circular base or turntables which revolve independently around a central shaft. Material can be stored laterally and the system suits ring-binders or lever arch files which sit comfortably in the wedge-shaped space. A single tier can hold twenty-four lever arch files. A suspended system is possible but jackets are purpose-made and are expensive to replace. They may fall off the suspension bar if they are not handled with care. Rotary units can be mounted in lockable cabinets to provide security but this adds significantly to the cost and reduces accessibility.

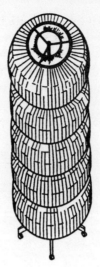

Fig. 5.9: A rotary unit.

'Times two' filing

With this system the filing unit is double-fronted, which provides a high ratio of storage space to floor space, and it rotates allowing the entire contents to be accessed from either side (see Fig. 5.10). The unit is pedal-controlled and secure when closed, although, in the event of mechanical breakdown, the records are inaccessible. Staff safety is also a factor. While the unit is foot operated care should be taken not to trap hands as it rotates.

'Times two' units have a shelf length of 30 inches (75 centimetres) and can be three to eight tiers high. Maximum advantage is gained when the units are placed directly in front of a wall as this eliminates the necessity for an aisle to provide access to the rear unit.

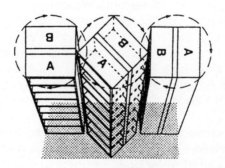

5.10: A 'times two' filing system.

Mobile filing units

As the name suggests, in this system the storage units are not fixed but may move across two of the three dimensions front-to-back or side-to-side. The major benefit is space efficiency, as the aisle space needed to access records is reduced.

Closed aisle mobile shelving is mounted on rails, moving backwards and forwards and compacting together when access is not required (see Fig. 5.11). The shelves can move manually or be mechanically powered. However, retrieval speeds are lower than with static lateral units and are on a par with the vertical units, achieving twenty-five to thirty-five items per hour. With highly active records, such systems would need to be considered very carefully. Staff have to queue to access material because only one aisle is available to work in at a time.

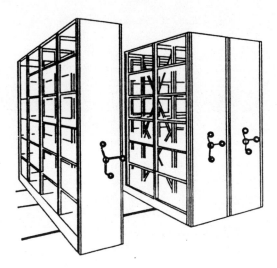

Fig. 5.11: Closed aisle mobile shelving.

Side mobile systems reduce aisle space by locating one or two rows of mobile units in front of a static row (see Fig. 5.12). Each mobile row has one less unit than the rear fixed row, and the units in these rows can be moved from side to side to allow access to units in the inner rows. The fixed rear row is usually used to store less active material. A variation of this approach allows for individual shelves rather than whole units to move. The front shelves move to right or left of those behind and the rear shelf pulls into the space provided.

Mobile shelving has some disadvantages. The heavy weight may give rise to floor loading problems particularly on upper floors,

Fig. 5.12:   A side mobile system.

access is restricted to one aisle at a time, maintenance costs are higher than for static units and it is possible to derail a unit. Staff need to be disciplined about moving material in and out, because if files are left protruding, they will be damaged as the units are closed.

'Power' filing

The vertical conveyor is a computer-controlled rotating filing system which uses height while overcoming the problems of access to the upper shelves by providing powered rotation of shelves to a single access point. The records are stored laterally in shelves which rotate through the vertical plane (see Fig. 5.13). A high retrieval rate is possible. A twelve to twenty-four level system allows 120 retrievals an hour as the files on the lateral shelves are delivered to the operator sitting at the access gate. It is obviously not suitable where simultaneous, multi-user access to material is required but the speed of retrieval is of great benefit in a highly active filing system. The staff productivity benefits can be expected to offset partially the relatively high capital and setting-up cost of the system.

Horizontal conveyor systems rotate either forwards or backwards moving through the horizontal plane stopping when the required section reaches the operator (see Fig. 5.14). If the power fails the operator can still access material by walking around the unit to reach the appropriate shelf. Again the staff productivity benefits can be expected to offset partially the relatively high capital and setting-up costs of the system.

Fig. 5.13:   A vertical conveyor filing system.

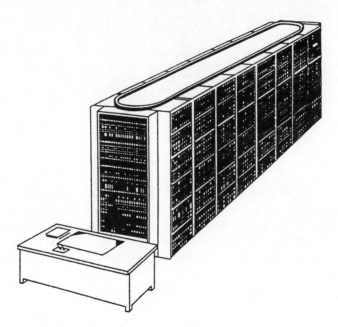

Fig. 5.14:   A horizontal conveyor system.

Centre column equipment

The records are stored in steel containers which are delivered to the work station or access gate by a centre column device – a mechanical arm or robot – which is computer-controlled and moves through the horizontal and vertical plane (see Fig. 5.15). The containers which are furthest from the work station may take some time to arrive. If there is a power failure manual retrieval, although not impossible, can be difficult as it means climbing into the casing and inserting a ladder. Higher maintenance costs can be expected and mechanical failure can occur, for example, following a weekend close-down of the office heating system which disturbs the temperature. Consequent expansion and contraction of the metal causes the rails and containers to get out of alignment. Greater storage density can be achieved, and again staff productivity benefits can be expected to offset partially the high capital and setting-up costs.

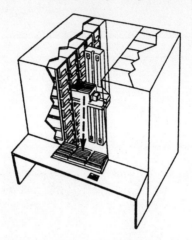

Fig. 5.15:   A centre column system.

The advantages of power filing of all kinds are the economic use of floor space and room height, and ease and speed of access. The disadvantages are the high capital costs, high floor-loading requirements and restriction to single access. Systems are also vulnerable to power and machinery failure.

The storage of non-current records

As with current records, very few organisations know what it is costing them to store inactive records. It becomes a hidden cost all too easily as *ad hoc* decisions are made to store material in corridors, store-rooms, attics, boiler rooms, cleaners' rooms, garages, basements and all the other odd corners which exist in every organisation. The consequences of such an approach tend to be the inability to retrieve valuable information; the physical inaccessibility of records; the retention of records which could be destroyed; increased health and safety risks to staff; the loss of records which have deteriorated beyond repair as a result of poor physical storage conditions.

Therefore, it makes sense to look at new and more systematic ways of storing non-current records, almost certainly outside the creating office. Naturally, records which are stored some distance from users cannot be as immediately accessible as those which are stored near by. Nevertheless, there is a beneficial trade-off between accessibility and space costs as the access activity rate of the records declines.

Out-of-office storage

This can be provided in various ways, most commonly:

(a) on-site storage in low grade office accommodation – for example, basements, storage rooms lacking natural light;
(b) off-site storage in low-cost accommodation – for example, warehouse space; and
(c) commercially operated off-site storage.

With all three options the objectives remain the same, namely:

(a) to achieve economy and efficiency in storage;
(b) to achieve economy and efficiency in retrieval;
(c) to provide a mechanism for the regular selection of records leading to destruction or permanent archival retention;
(d) to secure the records against unauthorised access; and
(e) to provide controlled environmental conditions to safeguard records from deterioration and damage from damp, dust and pests.

Several questions need to be asked. What type and volume of records are to be stored? Under what conditions should the records be stored? What level of service is required? What is the frequency and, to some extent, the urgency of access to the records?

The answer to these questions will determine whether on-site, off-site or commercial storage is chosen for the maintenance of non-current records.

On-site storage

The great advantage of on-site storage is that it is more easily accessible to users with a faster retrieval time. The disadvantage is that accommodation is often limited and there may not be the capacity to store all non-current records. If the staff who operate the on-site store are the same as the staff who manage current records there may, at times, be a conflict of priorities, so that the duties relating to the maintenance of the non-current records are neglected. Storage areas which are graded as unsuitable for office occupation may look attractive for records storage and appear to be low-cost or cost-free. However, these areas are increasingly being given added value as conversion could provide a new computer room, conference facilities or, underneath a modern office block, a car-parking facility. Basement areas may be considered and although some may be suitable, many will not because of poor environment, damp, temperature variations, dust, pests and flooding. Security is more difficult to guarantee in basements where access for maintenance staff must be provided.

Off-site storage

This may provide the opportunity to centralise the storage of non-current records and offer the benefits of economies of scale and rationalisation of procedures. Better storage conditions and security can usually be provided in a dedicated building using specialist staff. The principle disadvantage is that the off-site store could be some distance from users and the delay in retrieving records may be unacceptable. However, there are many records within an organisation which have a low level of activity and which are unlikely to be required urgently. Such records could well be stored off-site. It is possible that in some organisations a combination of on-site and off-site storage, providing intermediate storage on-site and long-term storage off-site, would provide the best solution. The activity rate would be the determining factor.

Several commercial off-site storage facilities exist in the United Kingdom. These companies provide basic storage and retrieval services for clients. Such a commercial storage company may provide a suitable alternative for those organisations that may not be able to justify an in-house storage facility. When choosing a storage company it is advisable to check the standard of storage and service offered. Listed below are some points to consider:

- The storage facility should be of sound construction and well maintained.
- There should be full fire protection with smoke detectors, extinguishers and, perhaps, halon gas for tape storage.
- The facility should be clean, dust-free and tidy with no evidence of insects or rodents.
- There should be adequate security with electronic intruder alarms and/or guards – access should be restricted to

employees of the storage company only. In some circumstances, depending on the confidentiality of the material handled, employees may need to be vetted.

- The storage facility should be conveniently located to allow for urgent recalls within, say, two hours.
- There should be adequate transport and guaranteed delivery in the event of vehicle breakdown.
- The delivery service should be regular and at convenient times.
- There should be an emergency service for urgent recalls outside scheduled deliveries.
- It should be clear whether specific files or only whole boxes can be requested.
- The customer's staff should be able to visit the storage facility and have access to the records.
- There should be insurance cover for the records in storage, covering the paper value only or the cost of re-creating the information.
- A certified destruction programme is often advisable.
- Whether the storage company supplies standard containers is worth considering.
- The storage company should employ properly trained and qualified staff.

Depending on how the records are controlled during their current life, information about the frequency and urgency of access to the records is not always readily available. It is sometimes advisable to keep, or ask to be kept, an activity log over a given period of time. Although it has the limitation of being a snapshot of the situation it does provide a more reliable guide to access requirements than the sometimes subjective reaction of users with no statistics to hand. These data may also be collected as part of the analytical programme described in earlier chapters.

As suggested earlier, knowledge of the activity rate of records is a critical factor in determining both their location and method of storage. With the decline in activity rate, the highest cost element in the storage system moves from staff costs to space costs. Consequently, the primary objective becomes the reduction of space costs. To do this, even greater space efficiency is required than in an active filing system and it is a key concept in the development of a relatively new model for storage in this country – the records centre.

Records centres

Records centres provide one of the most efficient and cost-effective

ways of storing non-current records whether they are in the form of
paper, magnetic media or microform. This arises from the effective
management of space, staff, security and environment. A records
centre can be operated on-site, off-site or in commercial storage.
The distinguishing features are the way that space and staff are
used to maximum advantage.

Space

Improved space utilisation and therefore cost reduction is achieved
by using low-cost accommodation and compact storage (see Fig.
5.16). Compact storage techniques involve a combination of high-
density shelving, random location storage and numbered containers. The type of shelving and the use of containers in relation to the
type of shelving is one of the main features which distinguishes the
records centre from other forms of storage. While containerisation
is not uncommon in archival storage, the use of containers to allow
random location storage and double, triple or more stacking and
banking of containers to improve storage densities is not so
common.

   The use of containers, for example, boxes, cartons, tubes and
tape cans, improves storage density as it holds material more
tightly. By placing loose files in boxes, space savings of up to one-
third can be achieved. Containers (which need not necessarily be to
archival standard) facilitate handling, thus saving staff time.
Records are kept clean, and random location storage is feasible
since each item can be identified and referenced to an individual
container and container location.

Random location storage

Placing containers randomly wherever space is available optimises
space use, minimises the handling of boxes and therefore reduces
staff costs. Sequential arrangement of boxes holding files in the
same file series is not essential as control can be maintained by other
means, usually the transfer (transmittal) or deposit list which
itemises every record held and indicates its storage location. These
can be maintained as a simple manual form or as a computerised
list.

   Unfamiliarity with the concept of random location storage may
lead to concern that records may be lost or that retrieval will be
slower and increase staff costs. Most people are familiar with active
filing systems where visual indicators or guides are provided and
users browse along the shelves until the required record is located.

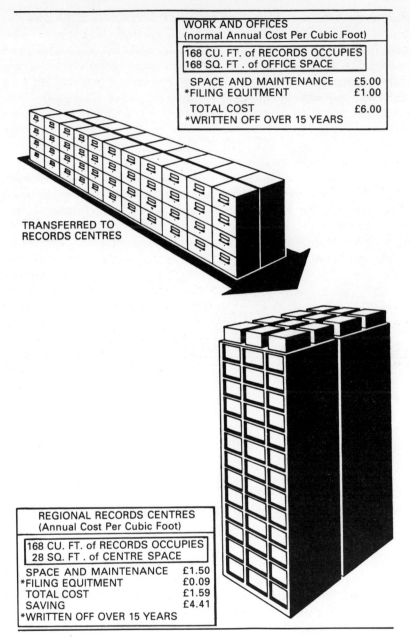

WORK AND OFFICES
(normal Annual Cost Per Cubic Foot)

168 CU. FT. of RECORDS OCCUPIES
168 SQ. FT . of OFFICE SPACE

SPACE AND MAINTENANCE	£5.00
*FILING EQUITMENT	£1.00
TOTAL COST	£6.00

*WRITTEN OFF OVER 15 YEARS

TRANSFERRED TO
RECORDS CENTRES

REGIONAL RECORDS CENTRES
(Annual Cost Per Cubic Foot)

168 CU. FT. of RECORDS OCCUPIES
28 SQ. FT . of CENTRE SPACE

SPACE AND MAINTENANCE	£1.50
*FILING EQUITMENT	£0.09
TOTAL COST	£1.59
SAVING	£4.41

*WRITTEN OFF OVER 15 YEARS

Fig. 5.16: How records centres save money.

It therefore seems alien and disturbing to find that records are no longer arranged sequentially and that a search through the lists of holdings is required before going to the shelves. Once the container number and location is known, retrieval can be very rapid and the system is no more vulnerable to misplaced files than more traditional systems. The recording of location information in the finding aids to the current system can, in any case, speed up access to the transmittal list.

If containers are stacked two, three or more deep/high then naturally access time is slower as containers will have to be removed and replaced to retrieve the required item. However if, as statistics suggest, less than 5 per cent of records which are over three years old are referred to then the staff inconvenience and cost is minimal compared to the cost of storing the records in higher-cost accommodation. Some records are very amenable to this type of storage, for example, audited financial records which must legally be retained for a total of six years but are rarely used. Such records could still be randomly located but consigned to the rear of the box echelon to reduce access inconvenience.

Pre-allocation of space

Some repositories choose to pre-allocate blocks of space or shelves to user departments. Random location storage could still be used within the pre-allocated block but space is reserved for the use of one specific client. This may reassure some users to whom clear delineation of territory is important and it may have advantages if a particular pattern of retrieval can be established. However, the practice does have some significant disadvantages bearing in mind the space efficiency requirement. Space may not always be available in the right place. If random location is not used, time and staff effort is wasted regularly relocating material to create space in order to maintain the physical integrity of the records series. It can also lead to a need to have at least 15 per cent of the storage space empty at any one time to provide the necessary flexibility.

Storage equipment

Shelves or racks should be designed to achieve maximum storage density. The nature of the building or room in which the storage facility is located will determine the type of equipment used. If non-current records are to be kept on-site in, for example, a basement area, then mobile shelving may be appropriate. Basements often have low ceiling heights with good floor loading and these two features would suggest mobile shelving. However, mobile racking is considerably more expensive in both equipment and engineering terms than static racking and consequently needs a high level of cost-justification.

If non-current records are to be kept off-site in, for example, warehouse accommodation, then static industrial steel shelving is more likely to be appropriate. Warehouses normally have very high ceiling heights, anything from 20 to 30 feet (6–10 metres) high, with solid concrete floors. This would lend itself to static steel shelving extending from floor to ceiling. Retrieval can then be provided by the use of mechanised handling or by direct access using mezzanine floors or catwalks built into the structure. Mechanical handling devices range from robot arms on tracks to mobile personnel carriers similar to fork-lift trucks. Both mobile and static shelving can be constructed to provide large shelf spans which can accommodate double or more banking and stacking, though in the case of mobile equipment there may well be weight and height restrictions which limit its applicability.

This allows even higher storage density reducing even further the unit cost of storing records. The average storage density in offices using lateral filing equipment is about 1.5 cubic feet (450 cubic centimetres) of records to one square foot (300 cubic centimetres) of floor space. In a records centre it should be substantially higher. The norm is 6.5 cubic feet (2 cubic metres) to one square foot.

Staff

Improved productivity is achieved in the records centre context by streamlining procedures relating to handling and processing of records, particularly their storage and retrieval, by the use of dedicated, trained staff. A small number of people can be capable of handling a very large quantity of records.

As already discussed, staff time is saved by pin-point referencing to the individual item within a container which can be accessed rapidly once the container has been identified.

Using the random location method new material is stored wherever there is vacant space. This saves staff effort which would otherwise be used relocating material to create space in order to maintain the physical relationship of the records series.

It is important that the content of each container is recorded on a transfer or deposit list. This is normally completed by the depositing department or office, which helps to generate confidence in the system and minimises the number of staff needed to operate the centre (see Fig. 5.17).

Packing containers

Containers are usually packed by the depositing department or

RECORDS TRANSMITTAL LIST—DATA SHEET

DEPT./SECTION CODE	DEPARTMENT	SECTION
CONSIGNMENT No.	FROM	DATE

GENERAL DESCRIPTION OF RECORDS (including dates)

CLASSIFICATION: ☐ UNCLASSIFIED   ☐ PRIVATE & PERSONAL   ☐ CONFIDENTIAL

RECORDS CENTRE USE ONLY		
Location Nos.	No. & type of boxes transferred	Cubic feet of records transferred

RECORDS TRANSMITTAL LIST   PAGE .... OF........

1. DEPARTMENT/SECTION CODE		2. CONSIGNMENT No.			FROM: DATE:				
3. Box No.	4. Departmental Reference	5.	TITLE AND DESCRIPTION OF RECORD		6. Inclusive Date From	To	Action	8. Action Date	9. Location No.

CONSIGNMENT PROCESSED BY ————————————— DATE ——————————

Fig. 5.17:   Records transmittal list.

section (see Fig. 5.18). Centre staff, therefore, only need to check off the boxes, and in most systems the contents, against the list to verify the safe transfer of material and then place the containers in the next vacant space noting the location on the list, a copy of which is then returned to the department or section. Again this minimises the number of staff required to operate the centre.

PACKING OF RECORDS FOR TRANSFER TO THE RECORDS CENTRE

(see RECORDS CENTRE USER HANDBOOK for full details)

TO ASSEMBLE BOX

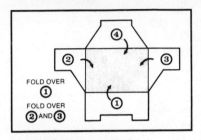
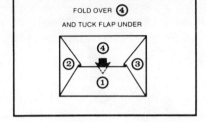

PACK RECORDS FIRMLY
Pack files upright so that file labels can be easily read. Remove records from bulky filing equipment (eg lever-arch and box files) and pack firmly in the box.

DO NOT OVERFILL THE BOX
There should be enough space for easy retrieval.

DO NOT FORCE ITEMS INTO THE BOX
Items which do not fit comfortably into the box should be made into bundles.

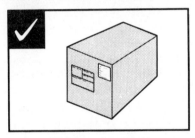

DO NOT WRITE ON THE BOX
Affix the Departmental Box Label in the top right-hand corner on the short side of the box beside the printed panel.

BUNDLES
Bundles should not exceed 10" in height, including string and packaging.

Spines of volumes etc should be placed alternately left and right to maximise use of space.

Bundles should be tied securely with stout string.

DO NOT SECURE THE BOX WITH STRING OR TAPE

OVERPACKING IS FALSE ECONOMY!

- ● BOXES WILL NOT FIT ON RECORDS CENTRE SHELVES
- ● BOTTOMS FALL OUT OF BOXES
- ● DISTORTED BOXES CANNOT BE REUSED

INCORRECTLY PACKED RECORDS WILL BE RETURNED TO THE CONSIGNING DEPARTMENT

Fig. 5.18:   Packing of records for transfer to the records centre.

Order of packing within containers

In order to minimise the staff effort required to identify and remove from the shelves material which is time-expired or is ready for review or destruction, each container should ideally hold material which is covered by the same review or destruction date. This also makes better use of space since a whole box space is released for re-use.

There are several methods of achieving this objective:

1. Material is placed in containers sequentially as it was used or coded during its active life and the entire records series is accepted. A single review or destruction date is established which is associated with the record that has the longest life expectancy. The disadvantage is that a great deal of material is likely to be stored for longer than is necessary thus wasting storage space.

2. The depositing department picks out of the active filing scheme those records which have become non-current and have the same review date. Several sweeps through the active scheme are made and each collection with a common review date is listed and sent to the centre as a separate consignment. There may be a disadvantage in that the records series is then dismembered and separated both physically and in the lists. This could be a handicap if it was necessary to reconstitute the records series either for retrieval purposes or for transfer to the archives.

3. Records centre staff sort through the deposit lists on arrival at the centre and pick out records with the same review date from the records series. These records series remain intact on paper on the deposit list with the physical separation noted on the list as each item might have a different box number. The disadvantage is that more staff effort is required to operate the records centre.

Selection of records

With non-current records there is frequently a tendency to store too much for too long. They are often kept in uncontrolled storage areas and destroyed in a haphazard way. This may be due to staff shortages, low priority or lack of awareness that records become redundant. When space runs out managers may take ill-informed, arbitrary decisions which result in potentially useful or vital records being destroyed in error. The real and often high cost of selection and destruction in this way is hidden.

In a records centre redundant records are destroyed systematically, with the agreement of the depositing department, using a certificating procedure. Systematic selection, review and destruction is a feature of the records centre approach which aims to be more disciplined than some of the more traditional *ad hoc* approaches to the storage of non-current records.

This disciplined approach follows on naturally from the work done in appraising records and developing retention control. This process encourages movement from office to records centre to archive or destruction, helps to predict workloads and to control the inflow and outflow material to and from the records centre.

Retrieval of information

There is little point in storing information and records long-term if they cannot be retrieved easily and with minimum delay when required. The records stored may have a low activity rate but the information they contain is still important to the organisation and has continuing administrative, legal and financial value. Consequently, the records centre should be viewed not as a repository for dead or useless records, but as a vital information resource which is an asset to the organisation. The quality of service provided is a major contributory factor in convincing users of this fact.

Finding aids

Users need to be assured that information held in the records centre can be easily identified and retrieved. This will give them confidence in the service and encourage them to send records to the centre as soon as they cease to be active. To achieve this level of service it is essential that there is an accurate record of what is held in the centre and where it is located.

The list (deposit, transmittal/transfer list) is the principal finding aid. It can be manual or computerised and is effective because it is simple to use. Its purpose is to record accurately:

(a) the title of each item or series stored in the centre;
(b) the location of each item or series by box number;
(c) the duration or retention period of each item or group of items; and
(d) the security classification or restriction on access, if any, placed on each item or series.

The list should reflect the way the records series was arranged in its active state. Although usually created by the depositing department, the list is kept at the centre in department order and an annotated copy with location number is returned to the depositor so that a copy of the finding aid rests with, and can be used by, both users and records centre staff.

The index is the secondary finding aid and can be held manually on cards or in computerised form. It is arranged in a different order to the list and provides an alternative means of access, for example, by subject rather than department. Since an index is staff-intensive and costly to create and maintain, not all records centres have one, although with the development of computer controls, the process has become less difficult. Some records series may arrive at the centre accompanied by an associated index and copies of departmental finding aids should be sought where possible. A simple method of providing this additional level of finding aid is the annotation of the filing index of the depositing department with the records centre location code.

Speed of retrieval

Users will have confidence in the system if information or records can be returned quickly to them. On-site records centres have an advantage in this respect. Records stored some distance from users cannot be as immediately obtainable as a filing cabinet in the office. However, with properly trained staff and the introduction of simple technology such as the facsimile machine, it is possible to persuade users to view the centre as an extension of their own office. Methods of supplying information to users can include oral transmission over the telephone, facsimile transceiver (fax) at two minutes per page, special messengers or dispatch riders within, say, a two hour radius, and internal mail service or Post Office within twenty-four hours. The level of service depends on the urgency of the request but the majority of users would probably be satisfied with a return within twenty-four hours. Naturally more rapid retrieval has a cost penalty and has to be justified against the potential loss which might be caused by any delay.

The records centre itself

The centre should be situated in the lowest cost location available to the organisation, normally outside high-rent inner-city areas and away from natural or man-made hazards such as rivers and chemical factories. It should, as far as possible, be self-contained though this may be difficult to achieve.

The records centre should provide reasonable storage conditions with a stable environment in order to ensure that there is no physical deterioration of the records. In some situations tighter controls may be necessary to protect more sensitive material such as microforms or magnetic tapes. This may require the installation of air-conditioning and improved insulation which would significantly add to the setting-up and running costs of the centre and should be reserved only for those few records which require such protection.

The records centre should be protected from unauthorised entry with electronic intruder alarms on doors and windows linked to a monitoring station providing 24-hour coverage. More sophisticated devices may be necessary if the records carry a high degree of sensitivity or value.

No smoking rules should apply in the records centre and as a minimum protection should be provided by smoke detectors linked to an alarm station. Relatively expensive non-aqueous extinguishing systems are available though fires in records centres in the United States have led to a reassessment of the previously negative view of the use of sprinkler systems.

In theory, the records centre should not need to expand once it is established and operating at optimum levels since regular records surveys and retention schedules allow for the prediction and control, in broad terms, of the intake and outflow of material. However, in practice, changes in operations and retention requirements will almost certainly lead to a demand for more space. Also a number of categories of records take a very long time to work their way through the system before equilibrium can be reached.

Cost

The initial setting-up costs of a records centre may be a deterrent to any change. However, compared with current expenditure on records maintenance, real savings from increased staff productivity and reduced running costs, and consequent recovery of new capital investment, can be expected within one to five years of its introduction. Some organisations directly charge user departments for space occupied in the centre, others fund the costs centrally. Direct charging makes departments aware of the actual cost of storing records, which is often hidden, but may deter use of the centre unless the control of records in current accommodation is very close. The method chosen will frequently depend on the normal policy of the organisation on the charging out of central services.

Overall, by applying these techniques, the cost of non-current storage, whether in a records centre or in other facilities, should be significantly lower than in prime office space. Considerable savings can be made in accommodation costs alone while improving access to information.

Storage of computer output

The advent of computers has revolutionised the office and has created challenges for records managers. One challenge has been in the increasing volumes of paper. Far from doing away with paper, many office managers have seen an increase in the volume produced by computer installations. Computer output can take a number of forms. Display of information on a screen or visual display unit (VDU) is transitory but data output to paper, microfilm, magnetic disk or tape and optical disk needs to be stored. Each of these media has different attributes and particular storage requirements.

Print-out

Paper records can be produced on A4 sheets which can be stored in the same way as a standard file but much computer print-out appears as bulky continuous stationery items mainly in two sizes, either 14⅞ inches × 11 inches (38 × 28 centimetres) or 14⅞ inches × 8½ inches (38 × 22 centimetres). While these are active records they need to be kept close at hand, but because of their size and bulk they present particular storage problems. While print-out can be placed in a cover and stored flat in drawers or on lateral shelves the most efficient method in terms of accessibility and space utilisation is to attach a collar or cartridge which can be suspended from a lateral rack. A suspended system is useful when an office has a mixed format storage requirement placing computer tapes, print-out and standard A4 correspondence files in the same cabinet. Inactive print-out, if it needs to be retained at all, can be boxed in specially designed containers and stored in a records centre along with standard materials.

Microforms

Direct output from computer to microfilm or fiche is a useful way of reducing the bulk storage of paper print-out and the cost can be justified if the records have a high activity rate and extended storage life. The operation can be carried out in-house or by bureau. Roll-film is produced on reels or cartridges. Reels of microfilm can be stored in boxes, either card or plastic, and placed in drawer filing units. Fiche or jacket fiche can be stored in envelopes, paper or plastic, which are placed in drawer filing units. The file drawers can be contained in any of the filing equipment described earlier – vertical units, lateral units, mobile or power filing.

In large scale systems with a high activity rate, computer-assisted retrieval (CAR) may be necessary. As with all microfilm or fiche systems, sufficient readers or reader-printers strategically located for convenient access by users are vital. One of the most common failings is that insufficient viewing screens are provided or that they are inappropriately located. For long-term storage or for storage of vital records which are essential to the running of the organisation it is advisable to store the master film or fiche in a secure, controlled environment, usually off-site. Dust, humidity and high temperatures can damage microfilm and the master set warrants extra protection. It should be used only to duplicate working copies as and when necessary.

Magnetic tape and disk

The usual output from computer is magnetic tape or disk. This may present special storage problems as magnetic media can be corrupted. Storage conditions which are protected from magnetic interference (such as the tube system of the London Underground) and which provide environmental stability within a range of 68–72 degrees Fahrenheit (20–22°C) and a relative humidity of 45–55 per cent, would be advisable. Tapes are best stored on lateral racks using either wire supports under the tapes or a suspended system. They may be in plastic containers, tape seats or collars, and cartridges. Colour-coding has proved to be of great benefit in the storage and retrieval of large volumes of active tapes, cutting down on the misplacing of items and speeding up retrieval times.

Contingency planning

The economics of operating computer installations and the risks and losses which could be incurred in the event of a disaster have given rise to an interest in contingency planning. Continuity, disaster, survival or recovery plans can be developed and various standby facilities provided – non-stop, flying start, hot start or cold start. It is worth considering off-site storage for back-up data so that any loss which might occur would be minimised. Such off-site storage may be viable as an internal facility. If it cannot be cost-justified, a commercial storage company could provide alternative solutions.

The Computer Services Association (CSA) has produced a code of practice which lists fourteen points covering the use of commercial storage companies, including security provisions, fire protection, timing of exchanges, vehicles, recording of data movements, staff training, customer access to premises and insurance. The code of practice is available from the CSA.

Optical disk

Laser 'write and read' disks are commercially available but as yet have had a limited impact in the United Kingdom although considerable growth is forecast. Since the technology is so new, standards have not yet been agreed and long-term durability can only be estimated. However, as a storage medium it is considered to be more robust than magnetic media, and normal office conditions without extra environmental protection are expected to provide acceptable storage. Optical disks are dealt with in more detail in Chapter 6.

ALTERNATIVES TO PAPER: MICROGRAPHICS & MAGNETIC MEDIA

GARRY TAPPER

Departmental support officer, Central Government Computing

Introduction

The difficulties experienced in maintaining and managing paper-based records systems and, in particular, the obvious cost of the space they occupy, has made the introduction of various forms of alternative media very attractive. Such systems appear to offer a panacea for the problems of records management. Consequently many organisations have set up micrographic and, more recently, magnetic systems as an alternative to proper controls on the production, maintenance and retention of records with expensive and, in some cases, disastrous results.

It is important that any conversion of records to alternative media should be undertaken as part of a comprehensive records and information management programme of the type which has been described in earlier chapters. The particular micrographic or magnetic medium should be chosen for its appropriateness to the function that the records perform and not simply to save storage space which in any case can almost always be provided more cheaply by high density storage of hard copy documents. The introduction of advanced or indeed intermediate technology, and a consequent change in medium, should always have improved functionality and performance at reasonable cost as its key objective and should not be used as an alternative to sound records and information analysis and development. The medium should also retain, in addition to the improvements it provides, the essential operating features and benefits of that which it is designed to replace.

If these factors are taken into consideration, there are enormous benefits in systems-based conversion of records to alternative media which should be used to the full in making records management more effective.

Micrographics

The use of microfilm

For many years microfilm has been a popular medium for storing records, particularly those that have little retrieval need but that do have longer-term intrinsic value. Microfilm has many benefits and some drawbacks and these will be discussed later. Microfilm is not usually recommended when records are in constant use, being regularly reworked, annotated, circulated or referred to. These types of record are best kept on paper or computer until their active life is over. It has always been assumed that once they become less subject to change then microfilm will become more relevant. There are, nevertheless, several systems currently available where microfilm is used actively. These tend to be very large record stores that have a low retrieval rate, randomly spread over the whole store. Usage of the whole system is high but the number of retrievals of the same record is usually low, for example, the total active file system of an insurance company or building society. Systems such as these have become more viable with the advent of the computer and its linking with microfilm files to enable indexing and automatic retrieval of the relevant record. Automated microfilm systems (CAR) will be dealt with later in this chapter.

Types of microfilm

Microfilm, or microform, as it is commonly called, comes in three basic types, based on width of film. These are 16 mm, 35 mm and 105 mm. Each of these can be produced either in roll or flat form and combinations of these film sizes and formats can be used dependent upon the needs of the application. This section will deal primarily with 16 mm roll microform, otherwise known as *roll* microfilm, and 105 mm flat microform, otherwise known as *microfiche*, which are most often found in business applications. Roll or flat format 35 mm film is generally used for micropublishing or for the filming of maps, plans or drawings in the form of *aperture cards*. The cutting-up of 16 mm roll film into strips and inserting it into plastic jackets to turn roll film into microfiche (jacketed fiche) is also commonly encountered. Similarly, the combination of 16 mm and 35 mm in jackets has been used in specialised applications requiring a mixture of standard A4 pages and drawings or plans in the same medium. Examples of such use would be in planning or architects' offices (see Fig. 6.1)

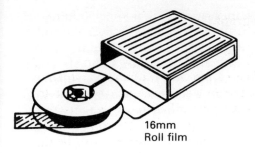

16mm
Roll film

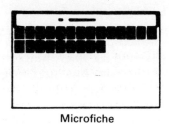

Microfiche

Jackets

Fig. 6.1: Microfilm formats.

There is also an esoteric form of microfilm called Ultrastrip whereby 16 mm roll microfilm filmed at a reduction ratio of around 20:1 is then refilmed at 10:1 and re-formatted into a 6 inch (15 centimetres) strip containing some 20,000 images at 200:1. In a carousel, over one million document images can be contained in a cubic foot. However, production is highly specialised and limited to bureaux, and the viewing equipment is extremely sensitive and delicate.

Microfilm is most commonly used in black and white although colour is used occasionally for certain specialised applications. Colour tends to be a good deal more expensive than black and white and it is difficult to obtain true colour matching. Processing and duplication is difficult to find in the UK and most is carried out in the USA or France.

When to use microfilm

Volumes

Microfilm thrives on large volumes and the more it is used, the more cost-effective it becomes, though hunting for problems for which to apply a microfilm solution to increase throughput should be avoided. This does not mean, however, that small volumes of records would not justify a microfilm system but it is always useful to consider where else it may be used in an organisation to gain maximum benefit from an investment, though care should be taken not to use microfilm for this reason only. Microfilm is well suited for clearing out and organising the contents of filing cabinets containing little or scarcely used files which need to be kept for various reasons, though a combination of review and high-density storage would probably achieve a more acceptable result. Most offices contain files of records kept 'just in case' and considering a microfilm solution may well help in taking the decision to destroy or severely weed the files. However, once a decision to microfilm the weeded files is taken, it will present an opportunity to organise records to suit the needs of the users, both current and future, bearing in mind, however, the need to retain file integrity. The requirements will differ depending on whether a passive or an active system is chosen and the main considerations of these will be the indexing required – fairly rudimentary for a passive system but somewhat more complex for an active system.

Retrieval

Rates of retrieval are an important consideration in the design of a microfilm system. Inactive or passive microfilm systems are simple to produce and maintain with rudimentary indexing. Library applications are good examples. Active systems need a good deal more thought. Indexing is the key to any system. It must suit the requirements of the user and there must be sufficient index keys to enable information to be obtained at least as quickly and efficiently as the paper system which has been replaced, though this can often be difficult to achieve. The number of index keys must be carefully controlled, however, as the effort to capture the keys if there are too many may well make the system unwieldy. In other words, if it takes less than a second to image a microfilm frame and several seconds/ minutes to capture the associated index data on computer, the indexing may be the undoing of the system. It is useful to use computer systems analysis techniques in designing this part of the system, paying particular attention to the needs of the user. If a database technology is to be employed, advice should be sought from computer software providers in, or external to, the organisation. Further information on indexing techniques may be found in the section on Computer Assisted Retrieval (CAR).

Audit

Microfilm has become very popular with auditors because of the inability to change, erase or extract information once made. Microfilm is often used in financial applications in roll film format and this produces a serial and often chronological record of financial transactions. This makes it a very acceptable medium for auditors. Examples of documents susceptible to this treatment are invoices, travellers cheques, bills of sale, delivery notes, cheques and many others.

Legal
Microfilm is now becoming acceptable to the legal profession since the advent of British Standard BS6498: 1984 – *Guide to the Preparation of Microfilm and other Microforms that may be required in Evidence* – which provides guidance on the use and production of well-made, properly certified microfilm as evidence, though it does include a number of provisos. One of the growth areas in microfilm in recent years has been in applications in the legal profession. The legal admissibility of microfilm is discussed more fully on p. 104.

Archival
This was microfilm's original and most popular use – film it, file it and forget it with the assurance that it will still be there, fully readable for many years to come. When made and stored correctly, microfilm's life is considered to be indefinite. Microfilm for archives is produced in most of the large archive institutions in the world such as the Public Record Office, the British Library and the US Library of Congress, usually as a distribution medium but also to preserve originals which have become too frail to be handled. Microfilm is often used in time capsules and recently a copy of the Domesday Book was made on microfilm in order to permit the rebinding of the original.

Applications
Application areas where microfilming has proved successful include:

Libraries – cross references	Roll or fiche
Newspaper libraries or cuttings	Fiche or 35 mm roll
Rare and old manuscripts	Fiche – colour?
Public utilities – maps and plans	Combination fiche or aperture cards
Patient medical records	Fiche
Purchase and sales ledger invoices	Roll
Delivery notes	Roll

Staff records	Fiche
Manuals	Fiche
Maintenance repair drawings and part numbers	Fiche/aperture cards
Company records at companies' registration office	Fiche
Payroll records	COM fiche or roll

The above examples are generalisations – as previously stated, the media best suited to the user's needs should be chosen. Fiche also includes jackets and up-datable systems.

Whether to use microfilm – factors

The decision governing the use of microfilm will include the following factors:

1. The value of the records and the information they contain. Is it really worth coverting to another medium? Microfilm does have a cost.
2. The use to which the film will be put. Too much use by too many people could lead to problems. However, the ease of duplication of microfilm may overcome contention difficulties.
3. The user's ability to use. Simple, inactive systems should not pose a problem for most users, although the general public is often wary of, for example, public library systems. Automated, active systems must be designed to allow the user ease of use.
4. The impact on other systems. Particular attention must be paid to other records-based systems in the organisation. Does microfilm already exist somewhere else in another department? Does the organisation have a computing or IT strategy? Ensure that the microfilm system will fit because records images will probably need to be integrated into IT systems in the near future.
5. Consider the cost. On the face of it microfilm appears an inexpensive option, but the costs should not be ignored and must be justified against the assumed benefits and alternatives. Will filming be carried out in-house or at bureau, with the additional requirements of control and management of records to and from the bureau? In-house operation will require a capital cost of equipment together with maintenance and consumables whereas filming at the bureau will be at a fixed rate per thousand frames, but of course while records are away for filming they will not be available for use. There is also

the cost of recruitment of staff if the filming load demands it and there will always be a training requirement, although some suppliers are usually very generous in this respect. Quality control in all systems adds a considerable cost.

6.   The existing system. How to get from where you are now to where you want to be is always a problem. Keeping the existing arrangements going while working up a new micro-film system will often cause problems and temporary staff may be required. Another very real problem is how to deal with the mass of paper already in existence. One solution is a 'day 1' system whereby from a specified day everything new is put into the new system and the previous records remain as paper files. An alternative is to film all the existing records so that everything is in the new system – commonly called 'back-record conversion'. This latter is often an impossible strain on resources but can be solved by employing a filming bureau. A more acceptable compromise solution is a 'day 1' with selective filming of paper files as they are retrieved on the basis that if they are referred to once, they probably will be again. The decision on how to proceed will again be based on the value of the records and information to the organisation and whether two differing systems can be handled for the management of records alongside each other.

Advantages of microfilm

Some of the advantages of microfilm can be listed as follows:

- has a relatively low cost;
- provides a relatively permanent record;
- creates a comprehensive record;
- helps to organise information;
- gets rid of misfiling;
- easy to duplicate/replicate;
- cheap and easy to distribute;
- easy to use;
- can be read anywhere;
- has well established standards;
- generally legally acceptable;
- established technology;
- stable vendors;
- provides security backup;
- space-saving.

Disadvantages of microfilm

These can be listed as follows:

- speed of production is usually slow;
- speed of retrieval is relatively slow;
- user acceptability – poor at first;
- back-records conversion can be a headache and expensive;
- low technology in comparison to computing;
- poor quality control produces poor quality system;
- difficult to integrate with other systems;
- photography can be intimidatory.

Many of these disadvantages can be overcome by careful planning, discussions with users, consideration of options, talking to existing users, consulting with academics, reading the literature objectively and *finally* listening to salesmen. Never buy the first system offered after answering a sales pitch. Always consider alternatives and take advice to find the best solution. Too many systems have failed because requirements were not closely specified initially and salesmen were the sole advisers.

Computer output microfilm (COM)

Input
COM has become a popular alternative to paper print output from computer systems and, as its name suggests, it is a means of producing microfilm or microfiche directly from a computer, by the means of a COM recorder in the place of a line-printer. Transfer of data from the computer to the recorder is usually via magnetic tape and, more recently, magnetic diskette. Both these are off-line media. COM can also be used on-line as a direct computer peripheral (see Fig. 6.2).

Output
COM output is usually on a standard 105 mm microfiche but can also be on 16 mm roll microfilm and comes in several forms to meet differing needs. As well as microfiche and roll microfilm, aperture cards using 35 mm can also be produced. Output from COM systems is usually confined to alphanumeric characters or symbols with very limited graphic capability. However, full graphic systems now exist, outputting either by vector or raster methods. Vectoring is a means of expressing graphics by lines and recognisable geometrical shapes. Rastering is a different technique whereby

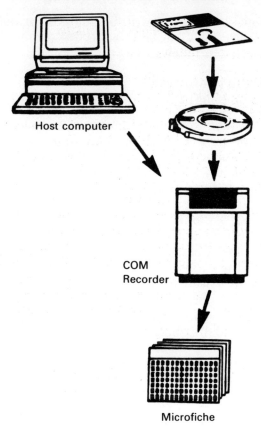

Host computer

COM
Recorder

Microfiche

Fig. 6.2:   A typical off-line COM system.

graphics are broken down into a fine pattern of black and white
dots.

COM output film can be either conventionally wet-processed,
silver-halide or thermally processed dry output. The latter means
that no chemicals are used but output is confined to positive-
appearing film and is somewhat inferior to conventional negative-
appearing output. Output is usually monochrome but very
expensive colour systems exist for specialist applications.

Production
COM production can be by either in-line or separate processing. In-
line, the film processing takes place immediately after imaging and
a usable microfiche is produced within seconds directly from the
COM recorder. With separate processing, the microfiche are
produced on an unprocessed roll which is then taken to a separate
machine for film processing. This latter system, although slower,

generally results in faster overall throughput for busy machines and can give greater control over the processing and thus a higher guarantee of archival stability and readability.

Benefits and systems considerations
COM has a number of benefits including the following:

1. COM is an economic way of storing computer output data. COM compares very favourably with paper by at least a factor of ten in material costs alone. The cost of production equipment is roughly the same when comparing COM and paper printers rated at the same output speed.
2. COM has a very fast production of output. At speeds of up to 25,000 lines per minute, a complete fiche of 270 pages or frames of information can be produced in 40–45 seconds.
3. There is a heavy saving on storage space. A standard COM fiche holds the equivalent of 270 pages of standard computer print output. There are techniques whereby far more information can be contained on a single fiche – up to 700 pages – equivalent to seven megabytes of data.
4. Replication and distribution is inexpensive. Duplicate fiche are quick and easy to produce (one every two seconds at a cost of around 10p each) and are very convenient and easy on postage – five microfiche can be sent through the mail for the cost of a first class stamp.

Images on COM fiche can now be easily retrieved using various types of automated system. A simple index downloaded to floppy disk during production of COM fiche can be used in a micro-computer or PC to indicate the desired frame on a fiche for manual retrieval. At the other end of the scale, COM fiche can be contained by the thousand in large, fully-automated devices which, by way of computer control, automatically deliver the required fiche and frame to a point at which they can then be scanned and digitised for remote viewing. There are several systems in between these two extremes, the most popular of which are based on automated retrieval units which manually accept cassettes containing around thirty fiche. Once the cassette is loaded, the fiche frame is automatically accessed for viewing and/or printing within seconds. Software for these CAR (Computer Assisted Retrieval) techniques has become very sophisticated, utilising the very latest types of database and indexing and retrieval routines.

COM is easily integrated into other systems. For example, it works well alongside conventional document filming systems producing fiche or jackets and can now share retrieval units and techniques. This flexibility is particularly useful when records are a mixture of computer data and paper (payroll, accounting, etc.). COM is already being designed into the novel technology of optical disk systems for both image and digital information. Raster or graphic COM is becoming well-developed and will ultimately prove an excellent output medium from optical disk systems, particularly where the remote printing requirement is for reasonably large volumes. Equipment already exists for this purpose.

Correctly produced and sensibly stored, COM has an archival life and image stability equivalent to conventional microfilm. This gives it better retention properties than paper in many cases. Legal admissibility as evidence is similar to that of any other type of computer output (see p. 122), though at least the microfilm image cannot be tampered with.

COM has standards. There is only one size and specification for COM fiche. It can be read anywhere in the world on the simplest of viewing devices ranging from a hand-held lens to the most complex retrieval, scanning and digitising system. The most important COM standard is ISO 5126 which is reproduced in Great Britain as BS 5644:1978 – *Specification for Computer Output Microfilm (COM) A6 Size*.

Operation

COM operation can be 'in-house' in an organisation where volumes are sufficiently large, or location or security dictate that this is most effective. However, there are several commercial bureaux operating throughout the country which will provide a quick turn-round service in mastering, duplication and distribution at very reasonable rates. These rates will depend on speed of turn-round required, whether delivery and collection is carried out by the bureau or the customer, distance, complexity of output, and, finally, the volumes or amount of work involved.

Costs

The costs of in-house COM production can vary according to the nature and size of installation. A conventional, cut-fiche system with low to medium duplication can be purchased for less than £100,000. At the lower end of the scale a small office COM recorder can be bought for about £20,000. Installation costs are usually minimal, normal computer power supplies are required and COM recorders can expect to be commissioned and operational within two or three days of installation.

Operating costs are low. Constant manual attendance is not normally necessary and is usually only required for loading externally produced magnetic tapes, where applicable, and disposing of output. Maintenance costs will be in the order of 10–12 per cent of the capital cost. Consumables, as with any system, will be an important cost factor, and film, both master and duplicating, together with chemicals where appropriate, should be shopped around for as the market is very competitive.

Software costs will be low or negligible, unless a large number of differing outputs from differing inputs or considerable changes are required. Normally software is written once for each job and tested by the supplier and the user. Job software can often be written as part of support training at the time of installation and used to accept the equipment, resulting in a live production system shortly after delivery. Further work can be written by the user or by the supplier at little or no cost. COM software, although comprehensive, does not tend to be particularly sophisticated or expensive to produce or amend. This is only true for alphanumeric COM; the newer graphic COM applications may well have some complex requirements as they emerge.

The legal status of microfilm

Those contemplating using microfilm for records storage are frequently concerned about its legal admissibility, that is, whether the records contained on microfilm will be admitted in a court of law as an alternative to the original document. Alternatively, would a VAT or Inland Revenue officer accept microfilmed records? In practice, records and information from microfilm systems introduced as 'best evidence' are used every day in courts, both civil and criminal. In the event of microfilm-based evidence being challenged, however, it may be necessary to substantiate it with some basic, good management practices. These are set out in British Standard BS6498:84 and include the following:

- A certificate of destruction of the original paper or at least the batch in which it was destroyed should be available for production, if required. Of course, if the paper record is not destroyed then it remains the best evidence and if challenged will need to be produced.
- An authority for the production of microfilm may be required. This is quite simply a statement from a senior person in the organisation that microfilm is produced as an established routine of the organisation's policy of records management and that the microfilm in question was produced as part of that routine.
- A certificate of filming may be required, signed by the supervisor

of the operation or the camera operator. In a good filming operation this should be carried out as a matter of course in that at the front and end of each roll of film there should be a signed filming certificate. Again this would be considered normal, good management practice.

Although there are other publications which are more specific to application areas, the main basic publication in this area is the British Standard. The Standard refers primarily to roll microfilm which is easier to certify at the beginning and end but does not preclude other forms of microfilm which could be certificated in other ways, for example, aperture cards which normally carry a signature on the filmed drawing, or microfiche where a dated signature can be filmed above each frame.

The International Standards Organisation is publishing a standard in 1989 which will widen legal admissibility to all microform types, with the exception of 'erasable', up-datable film.

Production of microfilm: equipment

Cameras

The production of document microfilm in whatever form requires the use of a camera. Cameras come in differing shapes, sizes and prices to suit the application. For large-scale microfilming of documents of similar shape, size and paper thickness, a *rotary* or *flow* camera can be used (see Fig. 6.3). For high-speed filming, at speeds of up to 10,000 items per hour, these cameras rely on the operator feeding bundles of single sheet documents to the input hopper which separates the pages and feeds the camera one sheet at a time.

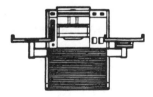

Fig. 6.3: A high-speed rotary camera.

In some cases, both sides of double-sided documents can be filmed in one pass through the camera and documents from the size of a small cheque to A3 can generally be accommodated. These cameras may suffer from paper jams or crooked registration of image if the operation is not carefully monitored, but as indicated they are capable of very high throughputs. For example, up to 100,000 cheques an hour can be filmed. They are mostly used for filming credit card and bank transaction documents, betting slips, invoices, football pool coupons, and similar applications where the documents are of a regular shape, size and colour.

The other type of camera generally found is the *planetary* camera (Fig. 6.4) which is used for the higher quality requirement single sheet feeding found in many office filing systems.

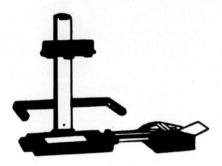

Fig. 6.4:   A planetary camera.

Single pages or bound pages from a file or book may be filmed. Some planetary cameras have a number of reduction ratios to enable them to film different sizes of document. They are the machines most often used in normal office situations and can be used with either 16 mm or 35 mm film.

Both the above camera types produce conventional, wet-processed, silver halide-based film which requires separate processing. There are also planetary cameras available which use dry-processing or up-datable techniques. These are particularly valuable when the use of chemicals in a confined space create a considerable problem – for example, in a small office without access to other facilities. Known as up-datable fiche systems because of the ability to add pages of information to an existing microfiche without the need for intermediate processing, they are particularly well-suited to applications where relatively small amounts of information are added regularly to a well-used record base spread over many records, and where the up-to-date information is needed quickly. Examples of such applications include press cuttings, insurance money and claim files and mortgage accounts. The dynamic up-datedness of the records is of benefit to the user in that the latest version of any record is immediately to hand. However, the image quality in terms of contrast and resolution is not up to that of conventional silver halide microfilm.

After production, copies of the master film are usually made to permit the master to be kept as a security copy while the duplicates are used as working copies or as distribution copies for external users. Copies can be produced very cheaply on a duplicator. These range from small inexpensive table-top models at about £2,000 through to large, high-volume, automatic systems in the region of £15,000. Duplicates are made on one of three types of duplicating film – silver halide, diazo or vesicular.

Silver halide is similar to original film and behaves in the same way by changing the polarity in the duplication process thus producing a positive-appearing duplicate from a negative master, which is not always desirable. It is the most expensive duplicating medium and needs darkroom handling.

Diazo is the most common and also the cheapest duplicating medium. Light-sensitive diazonium salts in the duplicating film are exposed by a strong light shining through the master and unprocessed duplicating film in contact. It produces a duplicate with the same polarity as the original. However, it requires ammonia to be used as part of the chemical process and this can be an inhibiting factor in some circumstances because of the unpleasant fumes that may occasionally escape.

Vesicular also uses diazonium salts in a special plastic layer in the film which, when exposed to ultra-violet light and heat, produces a duplicate on contact with the master film. Vesicular film, however, changes the polarity of the duplicating film in the process, producing positives from negative originals. It is slightly more expensive than diazo but requires no chemicals in the process. It is, unfortunately, not as stable as diazo and can only be used in normal lighting conditions for short periods.

After production and duplication, microfilm systems will usually involve active reference to the film. Even a purely archival system will require reading of the microfilm at some stage. Production of paper copies of selected frames may also be required, if access to the record is needed at more than one point. Next to the ability to find the required records, these aspects of the system are probably the most important to the user and if they are not specified and implemented to suit fully the user's needs, the system will certainly not function as efficiently as intended and may even fail completely.

Readers

Readers of all types are available to provide access to the various formats of microfilm (see Fig. 6.5). Several considerations will need to be made during selection such as:

(a) the need for front or back projection;

(b) negative or positive image;
(c) reduction ratio and magnification factor;
(d) screen size and orientation; and finally
(e) cost.

Fiche Reader

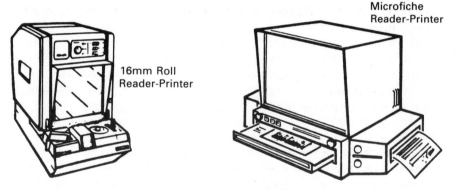

16mm Roll
Reader-Printer

Microfiche
Reader-Printer

Fig. 6.5:   Microfilm readers and reader-printers.

It is important to try out different types of reader to find the best
suited for the task. A useful British Standard is BS 4191:1976 which
specifies the essential and desirable characteristics of microfilm
readers. Another more technical Standard which may be useful in
helping to choose a reader is BS 6354:1983 – *British Standard Method
for Measuring the Screen Luminance, Contrast and Reflectance of
Microform Readers.*

Readers are not expensive. Simple microfiche readers start in
price at around £100 and rollfilm readers at around £750. However,

the cheapest may not always be the most suitable. They are certainly sufficient for occasional reference to the microfilm but in an active system, functionality should be given a higher priority than price.

If paper prints are required from microfilm, these are easy and cheap to produce, normally on plain paper. A large range of equipment exists for this purpose using conventional photocopying techniques and procedures. Typical costs of *reader/printers* are:

16 mm rollfilm (motorised)	£2,200
microfiche	£1,500
aperture card (A2 to A0)	£4,500 to £15,000

Production of microfilm: quality considerations

A well-organised in-house installation should follow laid-down routine procedures to ensure the microfilm produced is of as high and consistent a quality as possible in relation to the input from which it is created and the use to which it will be put. These procedures, known as quality control, should be designed to ensure:

(a) background density of film is consistent and within fixed tolerances;
(b) images are of adequate resolution;
(c) images are correctly positioned and not overlapping;
(d) microfilm is in good condition and without scratches or dirty marks; and
(e) image permanence has been achieved, if required.

Simple tests can be used to check these requirements and, in the case of the first four, checks should be made in-house as a matter of routine on every roll of film or microfiche, directly after production. For the archival permanence test, processed film samples should be sent at regular intervals to a laboratory equipped to carry out the necessary tests. Rules and useful guidance on quality control can be found in the following British Standards:

BS 1153:1975	*Recommendations for the Processing and Storage of Silver-gelatin type Microforms;*
BS 4187	*Specification for Microfiche;*
BS 4210	*Specification for 35 mm Microcopying of Technical Drawings;*
BS 5444:1977	*Recommendations for the Preparation of Copy for Microcopying.*

Where to produce: in-house or bureau?

Microfilm production can be in-house if the necessary staff, space and financial resources are available and can be justified. If for any reason it is not possible to undertake filming in-house, there are many commercial bureaux, frequently equipped to carry out the most specialised microfilming and there is almost certain to be one near enough to make the option of having records filmed at a bureau possible. There are a number of factors to be considered, however. The records will not be readily available while away for filming, and a bureau's security will not be as good as your own. However, most bureaux employ safeguards to protect records and, unless a very high degree of security is required, will provide a secure service. Quality standards must be monitored in a similar way to an in-house system. It is not sufficient to file away bureau-produced microfilm assuming it has been correctly produced. Random spot checks should be made to ensure that the microfilm returned matches the records sent in terms of number of frames or pages, that the images are readable, that the microfilm is archivally stable if specified, and that any indexes produced are accurate. However, most, if not all, bureaux will do a good job if it is carefully specified and monitored. The emphasis should be on cost-effectiveness. The cheapest solution will almost certainly not be the most effective since something will have been eliminated to reduce the cost. Microfilm bureaux are very competitive and it pays to shop around, but remember, the further away the bureau, the further your records have to travel.

It is not easy to compare bureau prices with in-house filming costs as much depends on the type of records to be filmed, the volumes and frequency of filming, and the type and format of microfilm chosen, together with the additional cost of setting up an in-house filming unit. However, in simple equipment terms, a small unit producing roll microfilm on a planetary camera and carrying out its own processing and diazo duplication would cost in the order of £20,000 to set up. On-going consumables would need to be added with film and chemicals for processing costing around £3 per thousand image frames. Bureau prices for the same production would be somewhere between £10 and £20 per thousand frames, tending towards the upper end if a quality product is required.

Bureaux can also be used for just part of the job – processing or duplicating or both. This ensures that control of the filming is provided in-house with the more technical and messy part of the job being done by experts. Remember again, however, that while your master film is out at a bureau it is not available for use.

A very useful publication which might aid the choice is the British Standards *Guide to Setting up and Maintaining Micrographics Units* – BS 6660:1985.

Computer-assisted retrieval (CAR)

The technology
In recent years microfilm suppliers have discovered and embraced the computer in its various forms. Consequently there are now some quite sophisticated computer-based retrieval systems available whereby both the indexing and the retrieval elements of microfilm systems are automatically controlled. Indexing is a particularly important factor with microfilm. The large volumes dictate the need to be able to find the recorded information quickly and accurately and the advent of the computer index means that indexing down to the actual frame can be maintained on computer thus obviating the need for laborious searching or browsing. The penalty, of course, is the need to choose the right system for the job and accurately to key or otherwise capture the index. Several methods and techniques exist. One very important question is when to index – before, after or during filming. The answer will depend on the system and various considerations.

Indexing
Indexing before filming results in having a computer record very early during the progress of paper through the system, providing a record of the information and its likely whereabouts. This can be of great benefit in dynamic records systems. However, it means that, after indexing and before filming, the paper record must be maintained in the same order as it was indexed in order to maintain the frame addresses during the filming process. All frames on a roll of microfilm are relative to each other and usually counted from the beginning of the roll. It follows therefore that the image frames on the microfilm must be produced in the order in which they are indexed. Similarly with microfiche, if the frame co-ordinates are entered during indexing these must be adhered to while filming.

Indexing during filming is popular in some situations, particularly where the index 'tag' is not large – a single number for instance. In this case, both the index and the frame address are captured while the document is being filmed. Frame addresses are produced automatically. Once the first address is input to the computer the computer will automatically increment the address with each click of the camera. The drawback is when there is a significant amount of index data. In such cases a good deal of time is taken up indexing, the film is a long time in the camera before processing and the records are, therefore, not available to the user.

Indexing after filming has the added benefit of providing a genuine quality check on the finished microfilm. However, constant reference to the microfilm can be wearying for the eyes, and a good quality microfilm viewer should be purchased for this purpose.

Other indexing capture techniques are becoming available, in particular the use of bar codes. A unique bar code is put on the document before filming and this can be read during the filming process. The bar code can contain sufficient information to be the entire index or simply be the key to fuller index data on the computer added before or after filming.

Turn-round documents, i.e. documents produced by an organisation for completion externally and then returned, now often have the customer details printed in fixed areas by the originator. This then enables the document to be read by an Optical Character Recognition (OCR) device during filming and thus index information is captured automatically. This system is used by the Vehicle and Driver Licensing Centre for all the forms sent to the general public for licence renewal.

It has to be said, however, that such indexing is more appropriate for the specific retrieval of individual, repetitive documents which are easily identified. The use of document-level indexing may not be effective in dealing with, for example, files of general subject correspondence (see Chapter 7, 'The future of records management').

Equipment
CAR devices come in several shapes and sizes depending upon the medium used (see Fig. 6.6). Roll microfilm is relatively simple to use. Once made and indexed, the roll can be read serially by an automatic device attached to a normal rollfilm reader which can count blips associated with frames or even the frames themselves. If the computer knows the relative address of the desired frame the device can find it easily and quickly – normally between five and ten seconds once the roll is loaded into the reader. Loading is normally carried out manually but large sophisticated systems do exist where the rolls of film are automatically loaded before retrieval.

Microfiche is not quite so easy to handle and fewer systems exist. However, the most popular type of system entails storing about thirty fiche in a cassette which is input to a special reader or reader/printer and the correct fiche and frame are retrieved automatically, again within five to ten seconds. Similarly, large cabinets full of

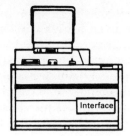

Fig. 6.6: Roll film CAR unit.

microfiche which can be automatically retrieved do exist in specialist systems, but these tend to have been purpose-built to suit the system needs. Large systems also exist for aperture cards which are somewhat easier to handle than microfiche. The cards are based on computer-style punched cards and suitable mechanical handling equipment exists for the purpose.

Software
The software used in CAR systems tended to be very rudimentary in earlier systems but has now become quite sophisticated, using PC-based relational databases for indexing and retrieval. The needs of the user must be carefully considered when choosing the correct CAR system, particularly the retrieval package. Once a system is committed to, it is difficult and sometimes impossible to change the indexing or retrieval criteria.

Videomicrographics
Other sophisticated systems exist whereby microfilm is automatic-ally retrieved, not for viewing or printing, but for scanning and digitising into document imaging systems, whereby images are captured from the microfilm which can be viewed locally on an electronic screen or transmitted for remote viewing. Known as videomicrographic systems, they abound in the USA but have been slow to take off in the UK and Europe. They can also be useful for integrating with modern optical disk systems where large volumes of back-record microfilm exist and where it would be uneconomic to convert to another medium.

Magnetic media

Digital (computer-originated) and image (document-originated) records can both be stored on any of the various forms of magnetic or optical media currently available. The type of storage medium chosen will depend on various factors which will include:

(a) the value of the records in relation to the cost of the media and the effort required for conversion;
(b) the volumes of records to be stored;
(c) the needs of the users and how the records are used;
(d) the amount of file activity in terms of additions to or retrievals from the file;
(e) the acceptable time required for retrieval of records;
(f) the type of equipment required to convert the records; and
(g) the capability of the existing or proposed computer system in handling the medium.

Digital storage

Magnetic tape

The most commonly used means for long-term storage of little-used computer records is magnetic tape. This has been in use for the last thirty years and with the passage of time has become sufficiently standardised to enable data on magnetic tape to be interchanged between differing computer systems, however incompatible.

Good quality magnetic tape can have a storage life of more than twenty-five years and, if properly maintained and regularly copied, data on magnetic tape can be retained for a considerable time. However, expensive in terms of both the media and production equipment, regular tape-housekeeping is time-consuming. A standard reel containing 2,400 feet (725 metres) of half-inch wide magnetic tape, recorded at 6,250 bits per inch, costs about £10 and will hold the equivalent of 30,000 pages of A4 size word-processed text.

Additionally, to be certain of subsequent reading of the data, at least two copies of the tape are usually taken and stored elsewhere. This provides security but trebles the media cost and effort. Magnetic tape also needs to be kept in a controlled environment, with even temperature and humidity and with high standards of cleanliness to ensure regular readability.

Magnetic disk

Magnetic disk is often used in computer systems for short-term data storage. This comes in two basic forms: floppy disk for small amounts of data which can be taken away from the computer, and hard disk for larger amounts of data, which usually remains associated with the host computer. Although useful for fast retrieval of data, magnetic disk is costly, so that most users transfer data to other media once its usage has lessened. Other media used will include magnetic tape, microfilm (COM), optical disk, cartridge (streamer) tape and digital cassette tape and even, in some cases, paper. The storage capacity of a magnetic disk depends on the computer system being used but will range from about 20 megabytes for a small PC-based office system to several thousand megabytes spread over several disks in a large, mainframe system. However, it would not be usual for mainframe storage to be available for records management purposes even in sophisticated office automation systems. One megabyte of digital storage will accommodate only twenty A4 pages of text, digitised and compressed. It therefore follows that 1- or 2-megabyte floppy disks are not worthy of consideration for records storage purposes, other than as a transfer medium.

Other magnetic media

Magnetic disk can be re-used continuously thus making it an ideal medium for transitory storage. Other magnetic storage media gaining acceptance in computer systems are *cartridge tape*, otherwise known as streamer tape, and *cassette tape*. Capable of holding large volumes of data, these tapes are generally used for the making of security copies. Like magnetic tape, they are written and read serially which can make retrieval somewhat lengthy. Cartridge tape uses normal half-inch or quarter-inch magnetic tape and a typical cartridge can hold up to 200 megabytes of data.

Cassette tape uses quarter-inch magnetic tape in a cassette similar to audio tape and large amounts of data – up to 2.2 gigabytes – can be contained on 166 feet (50 metres) of tape. A gigabyte is 1,000 megabytes.

Typical media costs are currently:

Magnetic tape	£10 for 22 megabytes
Cartridge tape	£4–£7.50 for 200 megabytes
Cassette tape	£25 for 120 megabytes
Magnetic disk	£300 for 300 megabytes

and the costs of production, reading and writing equipment are high.

Optical storage

Optical technology

Optical storage is currently confined to disks although optical tape and optical paper are currently under development (see page 126).

Optical disks currently differ from magnetic disks in the method of reading and writing data. A laser is used rather than a magnetic read/write head which makes retrieval from optical disk somewhat slower, because the laser read head is required to be further from the disk. Similar data formats and structures are employed in both media and therefore data can be exchanged between the two types.

Optical disks are now being used for long-term permanent storage of digital data because, once written to the disks currently on offer, known as WORM (Write Once Read Many), data cannot be changed (see Fig. 6.7). Erasable or re-writable disks have recently been developed and as these become more widely used one of the important advantages in text-based applications will disappear, i.e. permanence.

Fig. 6.7:   Optical disk.

Another type of optical disk which will be encountered is CD-ROM, Compact Disk – Read Only Memory, a development of the popular audio compact disk (CD). CD-ROMs can hold large quantities of published information such as encyclopaedias, manuals, parts lists and directories but as the disks are produced commercially by micro-publishers and the like, they will be only of interest to the records manager as an information source and not as a means of data storage.

WORM optical disks can hold large quantities of data which can be retrieved relatively quickly at random from the disk, and in image systems they are becoming a viable alternative to microfilm as a storage medium, whereas in data processing they are used as an alternative to magnetic tape or disk. Optical disks come in several sizes with differing capacities. The smaller disks are similar to floppy disks and compact disks, while the larger ones are similar to gramophone records. Thus we have 3.5 inch, 5.25 inch, 8 inch, 12 inch and 14 inch (10, 13, 20, 30 and 35.5 centimetre) disks on offer, with a few other intermediate sizes occasionally being tried. The stated size relates to the diameter of the disk and is usually proportional to the amount of data it can contain. The capacities of optical disks range from around 600 megabytes per disk for a small

PC-based 5.25 inch system, to several hundred gigabytes available in a large juke-box filled with 12 inch disks. As disks are exchangeable, the systems capacity is unlimited.

Systems considerations
A real problem of having so much storage capability is the effort required to capture the relevant data. If the data is already in the computer then there is no difficulty in copying it to optical disk (see Fig. 6.8). The problem invariably arises with image capture from paper. As in any imaging system paper is not such an easy medium to work with. It needs to be arranged, organised, sorted, de-stapled and handled, all before the image can be captured. This has proved to be one of the biggest problem areas, together with indexing, in several large systems currently under development. It is very much the area which should be left to the records managers to organise and control.

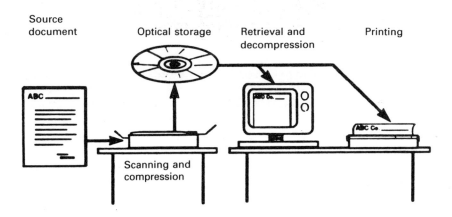

Fig. 6.8:   A simple optical disk system.

Advantages of optical storage stystems

Volume
The potential advantages of optical disk storage and retrieval systems are relatively easy to comprehend. Having so much information currently to hand has positive benefits in busy offices where large volumes of documents are dealt with, and speed and service is of the essence. However, there are clear management problems in having too much information available for too long.

Access

Multiple access to the same files and even documents within a file without requiring to make and distribute copies overcomes problems of paper filing systems such as:

- papers out of file;
- file with someone else;
- file not current or complete;
- misfiling and refiling;
- duplication of files required because of access or privacy.

Rapid access to a large document base is a further benefit, saving time and effort in searching for and handling files.

Security

Because of optical disk's inherent write-once non-erasable memory, a high degree of security is provided. Once an image is recorded on the disk, it cannot be changed. Any annotations will not alter the document but be stored as a series of logical information layers thus providing an audit trail of modifications and amendments.

Space saving

This is an obvious benefit. A sixty-four-disk juke-box could hold the equivalent contents of 340 filing cabinets in the space of just two of these cabinets. However, the cost of such a juke-box would be very high.

Flexibility

Optical disk systems can handle a wide range of inputs including normal office documents (handwritten or typewritten), diagrams, pictures and photographs. Even voice recordings could be stored on disk.

Transmission

Images can be transmitted to local or remote locations either through electronic mail systems or through facsimile links.

Windowing

Systems also have the ability to display multiple images or even parts of images on a single screen through a system of windowing. Composites can be built up from several images but the originals are always retained complete and unaltered on the disk. Information from a different computer system can be displayed against relevant images and integral word processing or desk-top publishing can be incorporated providing a total correspondence input, storage, retrieval and output system.

Disadvantages of optical storage systems

Standards
A media standard for 5.25 inch disks is in preparation but a standard for the 12 inch disk is a long way off. Recording and formatting standards are in the very early stages of production and suppliers tend to create their own, often hoping to create single-vendor, industry standards.

Vendor dropout
In common with any new technology, both hardware and system suppliers have already dropped out of the market after not achieving early commercial success.

Archival life
Although the claimed archival life of optical disks has risen in recent years from ten through to twenty or thirty years, a recent claim has been made for a life of 100 years. This is difficult to substantiate and such a claim may well place the technology in disrepute. Longevity is not considered a necessity for this medium as a good housekeeping routine of regular copying will ensure the longevity of the data and when erasable disks appear their use for copying and recopying will be ideal for computer applications. A greater problem over the years will be the ability to find equipment on which to play disks as the market, the technology and the software progresses leaving some aspects obsolete. This is a common problem in the use of computer recording systems for anything more than short-term storage.

Communications
This is a very real problem which will only be solved when very high rates of communication are made available. The amount of digital data produced by a single page can be up to 0.5 megabyte and at current data rates can take an inordinate amount of time to transmit. The advent of fibre-optic cable will ease the problem but already systems are taking longer than fifteen seconds to pass single pages of information to users, a time which is clearly unacceptable and not cost-effective, particularly if a large number of items needs to be accessed – a common requirement in correspondence-based systems, for example.

Legality

The legality of optical disk has yet to be put to the test, though as a
direct computer output medium it suffers from the same problems
as other computer records (see page 122). The ability to manipulate
information while in temporary store, either during input to or
output from the disk, presents a potential legal admissibility
problem. It is true that with WORM disks once an image is written
to the disk, it cannot be altered but the problem of alteration during
input or output remains. Systems are being designed to safeguard
against such manipulation but this will of course reduce the
functionality of the medium.

Indexing

Indexing is the key to all good image-based records systems and is
particularly important with optical disk, where if an error is made in
an index key, the information may be lost on the disk forever.
Indexing is an overhead and the depth to which it is carried out
depends on the amount of data necessary to enable the user to find
the required information with ease. These data are usually
captured manually by key-punching and verifying separately, and
can often best be done direct from the image in buffer store after
scanning, and before committing to disk. This will also give a
degree of quality control as the operator can reject poor quality
images which can be re-input before final placement on the optical
disk.

   Other methods of index capture are being devised. Based on
Optical Character Recognition (OCR) techniques, they currently
require OCR-readable characters in fixed positions on the page
which can be read during scanning. Very sophisticated software is
being devised which will recognise key words in text which will then
automatically be used for indexing without any manual effort.

Scanning

Other problems arising during scanning will be those relating to
the quality of the originals. This is not quite such a problem as
with microfilm because the spectral sensitivity of a scanner is less
acute than that of a camera and its functions can be more easily
manipulated to deal with poor contrast documents or varying
degrees of shading. There will, however, always be a problem
with coloured background paper and with very fine print if the
wrong resolution has been chosen. It will often be necessary with
difficult documents to scan them several times at different
settings in order to obtain an optimum result. Typical resolution
rates would be:

Normal office documents – A4, A5	200 pixels/inch
Fine print documents, reports	300 pixels/inch
Fine line drawings	400 pixels/inch
Fine detailed maps	over 600 pixels/inch

These are not hard and fast rules and standards in this area do not yet exist. However, it will be necessary at the outset to ascertain the optimum resolution rate before purchase of a scanner. It is not sufficient to choose the highest rate as storage requirements rise geometrically in relation to the resolution. Pixels are an expression of resolution and denote picture elements, that is, the fine black and white dots to which documents are broken down during scanning. The process is known as digitising, whereby black pixels are given the digital value 1, and white pixels the digital value of 0 (zero).

Software
Software is still relatively rudimentary and typical systems tend to be based on off-the-shelf packages around which the user has to tailor the system. As the areas of image handling and records management grow closer and more systems are applied, software is becoming more sophisticated, offering the end user more function-ality and ability to utilise his image database more effectively. However, the problems identified by Carl Newton in Chapter 7 apply to this technology as much as to any other records handling system.

Applications
Application areas where optical disks are now being used are those with large quantities of data, any of which might be required at very short notice by a large number of users. Typical systems starting to emerge are:

- newspaper cuttings library – information needed quickly by several journalists from a very large historical file;
- insurance files – the paper files of a society all available on-line for immediate access;
- building society mortgage deeds – similar to insurance where all mortgagee details are considered to be current;
- control systems for large numbers of engineering drawings;
- police fingerprint and photographic files;
- revenue file processing in USA;
- transaction processing at US credit companies; and
- correspondence systems linking imaged input with word-processed replies.

Costs

Systems costs

A typical PC-based stand-alone system could cost between £15,000 and £25,000. For this the user gets an IBM PC AT compatible terminal with high resolution screen, A4 scanner, laser printer and single 5.25 inch optical disk player. Image processing software will also be supplied but this will not be tailored to the specific requirement.

On a wider scale, an office-based or distributed system with eight user screens using 12 inch disks and linked via an Ethernet network would cost about £96,000. The price of a large corporate system, based on a central juke-box holding sixty-four optical disks and upwards, would start at around £250,000. A large core processor with several megabytes of main memory and a large amount of backing store would be necessary to handle the volume of images held. Several optical drives may be built in to the juke-box to overcome the problems of contention of several users attempting to access the same optical disk at the same time.

Media costs

A 5.25 inch disk in 1989 costs about £140 and a 12 inch disk in the region of £400. These prices are certain to fall in real terms as systems proliferate and the fixed costs of production come down.

The legal status of computer records

Despite the provisions of the Civil Evidence Act 1968 and the Police and Criminal Evidence Act 1984 the position regarding the use of machine-readable and computer-generated documents in evidence remains uncertain. This applies equally to printed micrographic or digital image-based output and depends largely on the volatile process by which such records are created and its remoteness from the transaction which it records. It is the clear link with the transaction of which they form a part that gives records, as opposed to the information they contain, their peculiar evidential value.

Much of the case law which does exist on the use of computer-based records as evidence tends to hinge on the technical aspects of admissibility – whether computer-generated records should be allowed as evidence at all – rather than on the inherent reliability of the information they contain. The laws of evidence are difficult to apply in computer terms.

Cross-examination is the primary feature of the English legal system. It has led, historically, to the development of a general rule that if a witness cannot be cross-examined then the evidence is not admissible. Such evidence is called hearsay evidence. Over the years the 'hearsay rule' has been adjusted to allow for a number of exceptions. This includes the presentation of documents, suitably supported by oral testimony or suitably validated, but under very strict rules. Since the documents could not be cross-examined they would be admissible as 'best evidence' and their weight would be evaluated accordingly.

In computer terms, there is little doubt that the problem is more complicated than it appears on the surface. Case law up to now has tended to stress the question of 'personal knowledge' of the matters described in the document put forward. On this basis records of internal computer operations, of which no individual could have personal knowledge, and which subsequently affect the output of the computer, have been deemed to be inadmissible. Nevertheless, the courts will inevitably become more liberal in their interpretation of the relevant hearsay rules in connection with computer-based material, if only because of the increased use of computers in normal business administration. If computer-generated material is not to be admitted, there may be very little documentary evidence available. However, it is important to recognise that the standard of accuracy required for court proceedings will be higher than that which would be acceptable in commercial operations. It is essential, therefore, that all computer installations, and all associated procedures, including rules for the retention of records, should be clearly stated and consistently applied at the earliest possible stage in the record/information processing operation.

Efforts have been made over the years to cope with the problems arising from the presentation of computer-generated and machine-readable evidence in criminal and civil cases. In many ways, however, these developments have left the law in an unsatisfactory state. The time that it takes legislation to come into being, combined with the exponential development in computer systems and the way they operate, has meant that the problems being addressed have changed substantially by the time the necessary law is in place.

On the basis of existing legislation, it now appears very unlikely that computer-generated evidence will be deemed inadmissible. However, some doubt has been cast on the validity of the provisions of this legislation, largely because of the way in which the software dimension of computer systems has been ignored. Although it may be perfectly possible to describe and certify the system as indicated in the laws of evidence, it is almost impossible to provide a comprehensive statement on the infallibility of the operating or applications software driving the computer 'at the material time'.

Although quality control standards in computer software have been much improved there remain doubts as to the total efficiency of such products, particularly in the microcomputer market. No software can be considered to be totally free of error and any claim to that effect should never be taken seriously. It is always possible that a set of circumstances may produce an error that was not discovered in the original testing procedures.

The physical problems associated with hardware remain. Breakdowns in the equipment can occur at any time. What is required, of course, is adequate knowledge and record of such happenings.

Weight of evidence

Argument in future will be on the weight, validity and accuracy of information produced in evidence. As suggested this is much more difficult to establish in an electronically captured and generated document than one produced manually in hard copy. Undetected retrospective amendment of computer-based records is undeniably easy and problems of verification remain. Who has all the information relating to the operation of the computer system, its software, peripherals and related storage facilities? Is it possible for any single individual to be aware of every aspect of the operation and control of the computer system? Generally speaking, a competent individual will only be able to provide such certification 'to the best of his ability'. The weight of his evidence at the same time must, therefore, be open to challenge.

Every precaution must be taken to ensure that, within these limitations, the system was operating efficiently and effectively and that any breakdowns or failures have been recorded. It is necessary to consider the legal requirements at the point of creation. Full operating records would be the minimum necessary to begin to satisfy these needs and it is important that records managers should liaise closely with the data processing department to ensure that such records are retained for as long as the records from the system to which they relate.

What is required is a good housekeeping system. It is essential that any computer operation should be well set up, well established and have comprehensive operating procedures. Every effort should be made to minimise the possibility of error, fraud, malfunction and corruption of data. This will at least ensure that when evidence is given it is the best available.

There are other problems. Data may be corrupted particularly in transmission over telephone lines from one system to another. In interactive systems with a number of users it is possible for data to be changed by one user, affecting that used by others. This is a problem which has been exacerbated by the development of microcomputing systems linked in networks and to mainframe computing facilities.

It is essential when setting up electronic systems to identify at the earliest possible time the final record in the system – the one which is contemporaneous with the facts contained – to arrange for this document to be 'locked' and for this record to be properly authenticated.

Even following all these procedures it may well be difficult to assert conclusively that the document produced is accurate and that the system which produced it was functioning correctly in all respects. All that can be done in these circumstances is to provide a system which demonstrably minimises the risk involved.

Image records in magnetic systems and computer output microfilm are equally affected. Both are capable of being manipulated, annotated, enhanced or excised during the input or output process and there seems little possibility of workable safeguards being introduced into these or other computer-based systems.

The future

Doubts have been cast on the future of microfilm in the light of emerging new technologies. In some cases microfilm has already been replaced by optical disk, notably in the field of COM. In the source document field, microfilm and optical disks presently serve very different work areas. However, optical disk systems are now being considered as solutions to records problems where microfilm may previously have been suggested.

Storage

Optical disk capacities are becoming even greater. Already a 5 gigabyte, 12 inch disk and a 1.2 gigabyte, 5.25 inch disk have been announced and densities will almost certainly continue to increase. New types of optical disk are being developed using different materials. However, as long as recording methods remain the same and formatting and labelling standards are developed and adhered to, new optical recording media should not pose a problem as the technology develops, as it should be possible to transfer data from one system to another, protecting the user from obsolescence. Magnetic disk capacities will also rise with the advent of new vertical recording techniques and new thin-film technology. Magnetic disk will probably win back some smaller optical disk applications as magnetic media is perfectly acceptable for short-term storage of images and has the added benefit of being erasable or re-writable. Already storage capacities of more than 1 gigabyte on an 8 inch Winchester disk have been achieved and this is certain to rise in time.

Other imaging media

Erasable optical disks have also been developed and will shortly come on to the market providing yet another tool for the records manager. With this medium it will be possible to read, write and over-write data on the disk giving it the same degree of flexibility as a magnetic medium. However, it will take away the assurance of relative record permanence which the WORM disk provides.

Hybrid optical disks are on the horizon, combining WORM, ROM and erasable areas on a single disk. This will provide one area of externally delivered reference information, one area for working temporarily with data and a third area for storing internal data permanently. Records will consist not only of image data but will also include associated digital data, and probably voice as well.

So-called *digital paper* is being developed which has considerable storage capacity. Two forms of this technology exist both with enormous potential capacities. The first is in the form of a 35 mm wide tape, 2900 feet (880 metres) long which, it is predicted, could contain the equivalent of 2,000 smaller optical disks or one billion pages of text. The application areas for this technology must be very limited, however. The second version of digital paper will involve the material being cut into disks, stored in 5.25 inch cartridges, and, like floppy disks, used in PC systems as interchangeable storage media. Unlike floppies, however, the capacity of the new disks will be upwards of 200 megabytes. The medium will be very inexpensive and will be a strong competitor to the smaller optical disk-based document imaging systems dealing with smaller volumes.

Other esoteric technologies being developed for storage media include one utilising crystal flow technology, which produces an updatable film which is imaged by laser at very high resolutions and can be produced in microfilm format or in 5.25 inch disk form. Volumes of up to 1.5 gigabytes per disk are being suggested.

Integration/hybrid systems

The growth of optical disk-based document imaging and information systems will be high in the 1990s as the technology becomes more accepted and more widely applied. Initially it will often be at the expense of microfilm and magnetic systems. However, as single systems become limited and the benefits of integration with other technologies become apparent, the use of integrated systems will grow. Examples of this are roll microfilm systems produced at the input stage and used to back up optical disk for reasons of security, audit or legality. Other examples are of computer output microfilm (COM) used as output from optical disk-based computer aided design/computer aided manufacturing (CAD/CAM) systems or office documentation systems for the same reasons.

Although optical media will become more and more widely used as magnetic media replacement this will invariably be confined to data archiving applications. The relatively slow response times from optical disks means that they are highly unlikely to be used in standard on-line storage and retrieval applications as replacement for magnetic disks.

CHAPTER 7

THE FUTURE OF RECORDS MANAGEMENT

CARL NEWTON

Director, Strategic Information Management

Introduction

A discussion of the future of records management has to start with the question – does it have a past? In one sense, of course, the question seems absurd. The literature of records management goes back to the 1940s and the classic textbooks, Leahy and Cameron, and Benedon, were published in 1965 and 1969 respectively. Neither has been revised and later works have tended to rely heavily on them rather than adding substantial new matter.[1] Even earlier, in 1956, Schellenberg had published *Modern Archives* which, despite its title, has some very important things to say on records management as a business, as opposed to scholarly, activity and is much undervalued as a contribution to the literature of records management.[2] In the last twenty years or so increasing numbers of organisations have appointed or designated staff to be responsible for the activity; the Society of Archivists formed its Records Management Group; the Records Management Society of Great Britain and the International Records Management Council have come into being; and the vendors of computing equipment and software have begun to use the slogan 'our product takes care of records management'.

Yet in another way the whole of records management is to be found in the future rather than in the past. All the works mentioned above were published before the impact of automation and scientific information retrieval began to be felt seriously. The undoubted growth in the number of persons designated as records managers by no means betokens any degree of uniformity in duties, methods or expectations. The societies have reached an apparent plateau both in numbers and in the issues which their meetings and publications address, and the vendors, by and large, appear to have no exact concept of what records management really means in practice – certainly their products do not 'take care of it', sometimes indeed they make it even more difficult.

There are five major issues which can be seen as of primary significance for the future of records management as part of the general development of information systems, some of which will in fact be likely to change the nature and objectives of records management itself. These five areas, which will each be addressed in turn in the remainder of this chapter, are as follows:

1. Planning and structured approach.
2. The relationship between records and data.
3. The application of records management to automated office systems.
4. Classification and indexing and the use of records as information sources.
5. The need to automate records management itself.

Planning and structured approach

The concept of planning for the development of an information system is not new but the application of it to records management, which is after all a key part of the creation of such systems, seems to be only dimly recognised at the moment. This is all the more difficult to understand given the frequent references to the 'life-cycle' idea in the literature. The view that all records irrespective of form and purpose pass through certain well-defined phases, each of which require special techniques for effective control, leads ineluctably to the conclusion that these techniques need to be integrated into a planned system. It must be assumed that such an approach will become the norm rather than the exception in the future.

If planning is a requirement then it is also necessary to have a structured method as a foundation for design. This has been proved by the traumas which have resulted from the design of automated systems without a structured method. A major consequence is the construction of applications which are deficient in meeting the business needs of the organisation and do not communicate effectively with other information facilities. If 'application' is substituted for 'filing system', or 'records centre', or 'microfilm programme' the same can be said of records management activities.

The information systems world (which means at the moment the computerised data-orientated world) has devised a number of structured methods to try to deal with the problem. These methods, in the main, have been copyrighted and are associated with a particular consultancy firm or even individual.[3] However, they generally stress the need to look beyond the immediate technical definition of a user requirement to the purposes and needs of the organisation as a whole. Also they stress the analysis of the activities and information needs and outputs, and this is precisely the area of strongest relationship to records management since information outputs are, in the majority of cases, records. Moreover records have always been recognised in the literature as having an organic relationshiop to those activities. In fact, the so-called 'structured methodologies', despite their modern image, owe a great deal to views of the nature of information which go back to the seventeenth century.

As has already been suggested, planning a records management programme must start with the business as a whole, its objectives, functions and critical success factors[4] and with an approach to development in which records management (equally with other disciplines such as database management and library science) forms a part of a strategy for meeting the information needs and controlling the information outputs of the user. In other words the business plan is just as much a vital preliminary factor in this as it is in any other information management development. Second, a picture of the organisation should be built up, by interview and analysis, of its functions, inputs, outputs and information needs. This is an important basis on which to design the structure, nature and organisation of record systems.[5] From the functions can be derived the pattern both of classification and level of support, while the relationship of inputs and outputs will indicate where overall guidelines or controls are needed. For instance, if several functions produce the same kind of record it clearly makes sense to provide the same approach to their management, even if the functions operate independent records systems.

Following a structured path there are four major tasks to be undertaken. These are:

(a) survey and evaluation;
(b) standards and procedures;
(c) records analysis; and
(d) records systems design.

Survey and evaluation

In one sense the survey is unnecessary but it has to be admitted that present systems usually provide valuable insights into what the organisation is attempting to achieve. However, it is important not to spend too much time on analysing the existing situation. Records management is a dynamic, a catalyst and vehicle for change, concerned with greater effectiveness rather than merely improved efficiency and the important step is the evaluation. This aims at highlighting the key issues, the opportunities and danger spots and sketches out how records fit into overall information strategy. Sometimes, indeed, it happens that an information strategy plan is the result of a records evaluation. One important issue is to determine how well records systems are supporting the critical success factors and which system actually contributes most to meeting overall objectives. (If an information strategy exists these two elements will have been decided already.) From this a general plan for record systems can then be prepared indicating needs, resources required, timetable, etc.

Standards and procedures

The next stage is to prepare the corporate standards and guidelines and the overall 'architecture' of the records management programme. It is important to stress here that however small the organisation may be it does require 'corporate' procedures (though this may only be one page) as opposed to actual procedural and operational rules. Since information is a corporate resource it must be managed at a corporate, as well as at an operational, level. The corporate standards, therefore, set out objectives, best practice and recommended criteria which are applicable in general to the organisation. They should cover such matters as the definition of records systems, document control, classification and retrieval, storage, storage media, retention, use of records, costing, security and audit.

The records architecture is simply a model showing what facilities are required for each function and how they relate to each other (Fig. 7.1). The main purpose of this is to ensure that there is a logical basis for the implementation of individual systems and facilities. Also at this stage the specification for an automated records control system (ARCS) should be prepared. More will be said of this later.

Records analysis

The third stage is records analysis which means examination of records systems to determine their content and to establish data about location, origin and information value. At this stage the

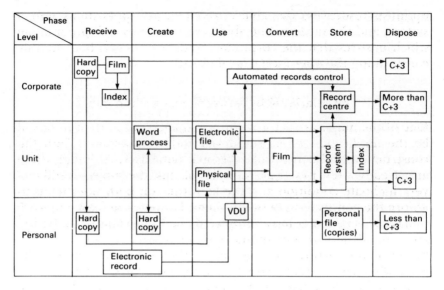

Fig. 7.1:   Records architecture. (*Source*: Strategic Information Management.)

criteria relating to retention should also be applied and at least a preliminary assessment made of probable retention periods. Where a full information strategy plan exists with data models, it must be possible to relate the records to the data which they support. Indeed this is an important step in integrating records into automated systems. At this stage too it should be possible to establish the security levels required.

Records systems design

Having established the principles and accumulated sufficient data by analysis, individual records systems can be specified. It is at this stage that the exact references, classifications, schedules and operational procedures are designed, which now can be seen to fit logically into a thorough 'top-down' approach to the problem. The importance of this is that it avoids the perils of designing, say, a manager's filing system, as if it were an independent function related only to the manager's particular personal need.

All this may sound formidable as an approach to what might be thought a simple problem. In practice, even a large organisation could undertake at least the first two stages in a few weeks and the records analysis can be then geared to deal with the areas of most business significance. This is one of the key reasons for having a structured method. The others may be said to include the ability to optimise resources, the ability to integrate applications into a system, and the facility to be able to secure an overall programme which ensures that the corporate needs are met without unduly constraining the operational level users.

The relationship between records and data

One of the major areas for records management in the future will be the application of its standards and techniques to both the construction and control of relational databases. Although there are already a few practical examples of this, the subject is still in a very inchoate condition and the literature on both sides tends to ignore the connections between them. However, at least one work by a records manager has attempted to deal with some of the basics[6] and a handful of writers on database management in fact refer to the need for records management without, however, necessarily using the term.[7] It is incorrectly assumed in some quarters that the construction of databases inevitably removes the need to have records at all. However, as James Martin has pointed out '. . . data needs to be structured. We must not group any old collection of data items into a record.'[8]

Even allowing for the fact that the term 'record' is used here in its computer sense, this quotation goes to the heart of the matter. Data is value-added; records remain the essential means of presenting information because of their structure and context. Thus the statement 'A owes £50 to B' has a meaning as data, but its operational significance is nugatory until it is presented in the form of an invoice, duly created according to controlled procedures as part of standard business activity. The medium in which the invoice appears is irrelevant for records management.

Using databases as records generators

If structure is significant then clearly a database must be able to reproduce it. This is relatively easy where the data items are of the same nature and in a clearly defined sequential order, each assimilable into a database without the need to have a physical record. This is the situation, for example, with invoices. Problems arise when a record is the result of a number of actions, some of which may take place outside the organisation itself. This is particularly the case where, for example, an application form needs to be signed by the applicant. Hence the signature is an essential piece of data but it is not easily absorbed into a database system. Moreover there are often legal considerations involved which necessitate the maintenance of the original application as an input.[9] If the invoice situation lends itself to full integration, provided there are facilities for the complete reconstruction of the record from the data in an acceptable manner, the second situation could be called 'conjugation' – the need to be able to join database and physical record in a meaningful presentation.

The third situation is one in which it is almost impossible, for technical, legal or cost reasons, to assimilate the record into a database. A map is clearly such a case, but minutes and technical reports may also fall into these categories. Automated indexing packages may be applied to word-processed text but the system overheads can be enormous and the indexing and structure still require management. Hence we have a situation where the best practical step is to supply an interface between the record and the database which enables the latter to identify but not replace it even in part.

These three scenarios are set out in Fig. 7.2. It is important to recognise that procedures such as retention must be applied to data-generated records as well as hard copy.

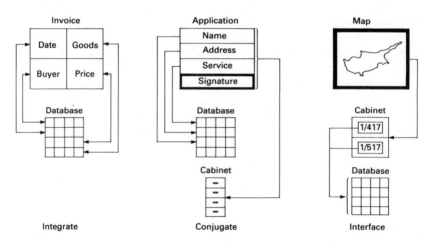

Fig. 7.2:   Records and data. (*Source*: Strategic Information Management.)

The database as a record

In all the cases we have discussed, the database is in effect a facility and as such presents a fundamental problem for the application of records management techniques. However, there are going to be, and indeed are already, increasing numbers of situations in which the database itself is a record. These arise, for example, where financial information is 'creamed off' from a number of trans-actional databases in order to provide management decision-support, particularly where it is related to data from other sources or areas. In effect this type of database is a control record in its own right and decisions have to be made about its management. The kind of questions which need to be addressed include, but are no means confined, to the following:

- Can a satisfactory retention period be applied to the data?
- If so, can the data be held for the set period on-line or will conversion be required, and if so, what is the best medium?[10]
- If conversion is required, can an adequate means of retrieval be maintained?
- Has a time sequence been built in as part of the design?
- If the data is subject to up-date, is it necessary to retain or record displaced data?
- Is the logical order of the database the same as is needed for a logical hard copy record?
- Who is going to be responsible for maintenance?

The last point raises an issue of some complexity. It is all too often assumed that the information systems department can make an independent decision on purely technical grounds. It has been stressed in the first section of this chapter that data relates to business needs and its retention and maintenance are *business*, not technology, decisions. In a 'traditional' situation it is fairly easy to establish both the origin and point of use of a record since there is a physical entity which can (in its original form) be in only one place at a time. A networked database which can be referenced and perhaps up-dated from a number of different points at what is, in practical terms, the same moment in time, presents problems of a kind similar to that propounded by the Greek philosopher Zeno about the nature of movement. Indeed we could say that there is a Zeno's Record Arrow (Fig. 7.3) which illustrates that an electronic record can be present in several places at once and leaves traces of itself in the course of its passage. This stresses that decisions on manage-ment are likely to have to be made in a co-operative context in future – a dysfunctional decision in one area could wreck the whole information structure.

The question of time as applied to databases is also important. It is often claimed that the power of modern relational database management systems obviates the necessity for a pre-determined structure and sequence. This is however only partially true. If I need to know the moment that a communication is actually received, I have to ensure that it is in fact recorded somewhere.

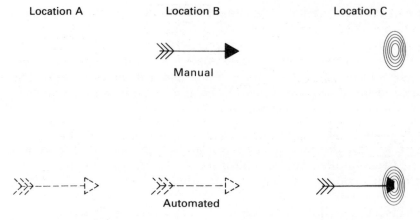

Fig. 7.3: Zeno's Record Arrow. (*Source*: Strategic Information Management.)

Moreover if I need to establish a relationship between data items, I need at least verification that the DBMS will provide that particular relationship, since it may not emerge from analysis undertaken at a purely transactional level. It has often been said that the higher the level of decision-making, the more significant the outside environment and past and future events become. In other words, the problems of historical and external data need to be considered as part of the management of a database as an organisational record, and it is certain that unmanaged electronic data will eventually be as great a problem as unmanaged paper records today.

The application of records management to office systems

In the early 1980s it seemed that the fully automated office was only a short distance in time away from fulfilment. In practice the number of office automation systems (OASs) actually 'live' in a working environment has remained small. The definition of an OAS is that it provides automated access, through a single-user terminal, to a wide range of facilities as set out in Fig. 7.4. A number of offices have moved part of the way towards this by, for instance, linking word processors and adding an electronic mail facility, but these are mere gestures and have little real significance for the records manager.

Yet the future is a different matter. There are undoubted benefits to be gained from the installation of good OASs which are properly specified to deal with record and information management issues, as opposed to merely providing communications and personally available computing capacity. Indeed the unstructured

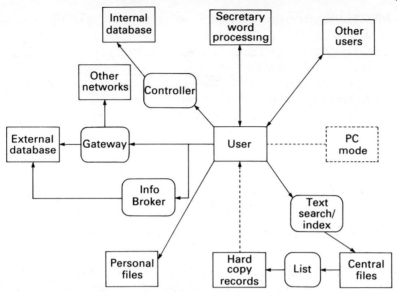

Fig. 7.4. Office automation information facilities. (*Source*: Strategic
Information Management.)

introduction of personal computers in one well-known organisation
has been described as 'the kiss of death for management
efficiency'.[11]

A wide range of issues are raised by office automation which are
intimately related to records management and these cannot all be
addressed here. However, it is important to stress that for the future
the successful implementation of OAS will depend very heavily on
getting the records management requirements right since it is that
area in which the benefits can be maximised. No implementation
team should be established without at least one member being
skilled in records management. An OAS is, in fact, a records system.

Specification

An office system needs to be related to:

(a) general information and records strategy;
(b) paper and film records;
(c) data processing systems and main-frame databases;
(d) public on-line data;
(e) bibliographic data.

The specification must include:

(a) file organisation and classification method;

(b) retention requirements;
(c) access rights;
(d) record security;
(e) search and retrieval facilities;
(f) control data for records management purposes and interface to an automated records control system; and
(g) interfaces to other records systems whether manual or automated.

A records management overview of the system should be prepared on the lines of that illustrated in Fig. 7.5. This should include computer 'archiving' and absolute archiving of records, the relationship to paper and film and the links to any other information sources required, and should be set in the context of the life-cycle of records.

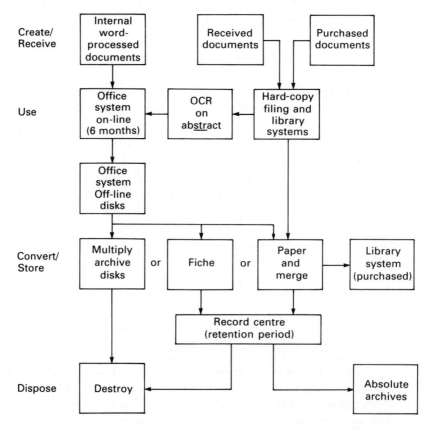

Fig. 7.5: A records management model for an integrated office system.
(*Source*: James Martin Associates.)

Records system design in OAS

The objectives are:

(a) to provide well organised series of records which will maintain their integrity as sources of information throughout their life-cycle;

(b) to integrate records held on different media into one comprehensive reference system;

(c) to promote efficient retrieval by employing automated search aids in a way which is responsive to records structure; and

(d) to promote effective records management by employing automated tools for collecting information about records for the purpose of control (see below).

There are two areas of detailed design which need to be considered: life-cycle management and overall records control.

Life-cycle management

Document creation
The issues here are as follows:

1. How should corrections to documents be allowed, by whom and in what circumstances? Also at which point must a record be regarded as final and the electronic version of, for example an out-letter, be 'frozen' in consequence?

2. In what circumstances can a common draft or pro forma document be created and how should it be held on the system?

3. How should the originator of a document be indicated?

4. How should standard texts used as templates be managed so as not to confuse the integrity of completed records?

5. What should be done to ensure that the revision and status of a document are always clear?

Document reception
This involves the following requirements:

1. The need to establish procedures for deciding whether to maintain in-coming paper documents in their original medium or to convert them to a medium compatible with the OAS.

2. The need to find a means of linking documents maintained on an incompatible medium to the system by, for example, providing a list or schedule accessible through the terminal and

identifying the file references of the documents, probably with a keyword index.

3. The need to work out a method of registration of in-coming documentation if required.

4. The need to decide where documents are received via electronic means, whether to keep them in this form and for how long? The storage capacity of an OAS is relatively low. Optical disk (see Chapter 6) may be a means of extending this capacity but obviously does not provide the same high-speed access. Moreover, there are problems with the optical disk as a mass storage device for records, as opposed to bibliographic data, which relates to the question of structure and context. Sheer volume, too, is likely to be a problem if no proper retention procedure has been worked out.

Document use

In this area the vital question of file organisation (here used in its computer sense) has to be addressed. A tree-structure provides a useful basis for the allocation of documents in a manner analogous to a traditional file system (using the word in its records management sense). However, an inverted file store giving random access can only be accessed by keywords so that (record) files have to be defined in terms of keywords derived from their titles.

File closure must be applied on the same principles as hard copy records, either by altering access rights, or by preventing it by the tagging of documents with a closed file reference, etc.

Disposition

This requires the following:

1. The determination of who is to be responsible for disposition archiving and absolute archives.

2. Where records are destroyed or transferred to an archive medium, the creation of procedures for ensuring that the OAS retains sufficient data about them to enable them to be retrieved when required. This includes the amendment and updating of control data.

3. A means of ensuring that record and file integrity are maintained when archiving takes place. Thus, individual documents should not be archived separately when they form part of the same transaction.

Records control design

The value of a record is derived from both context and content. It is essential to preserve both these attributes in any records system. It has been suggested that text retrieval systems should be applied as an integral part of OAS.[12] However, as these operate mainly on the principle of keyword search they have severe limitations when applied to the control of records. For one thing text retrieval is dependent on memory and personal recognition. Thesauri are very difficult to construct for records, and intensive word recognition systems produce an unmanageably large number of recalls, unless controlled by an appropriate arrangement and classification. An OAS must therefore have retrieval paths which are based on customary working practices and recall methods derived from adequate records structuring.

The problem is further compounded, at the moment, by the lack of adequate control features for records management in currently available office systems. This means that special steps have to be taken to use features for the purpose of control with sometimes less than elegant results. Office systems are document- not series-orientated, and usually provide no file structure (in the records management sense) or data relating to records which are not integrated electronically to the system itself, for example archives. These are factors which have to be built in somehow in the way the system is configured at its inception.

Retention is still an important factor in office systems. It has to be realised that the principles are not changed by automation and records should not be kept longer than necessary simply because there appears to be minimal cost in so doing. The following practical steps at least are required:

1. The retention period must appear as a prompt for the user when selecting the file reference to be applied.
2. The medium most appropriate to the length and purpose of retention has to be selected. It must be accepted that this can mean conversion to film, or even to paper.
3. If microfilm or optical disk systems are used for long-term records, maintenance and expansion capacity have to be planned.

The future of records management will be closely linked with the development of office automation.

Records as information sources

Classification, retention and indexing

The management of records as presentations of structured data involves the provision of adequate means of access to them, particularly in series but also, where appropriate, to individual items. It is important to realise that an individual record gains as an information source from organic relationships with other records arising from the same activity or transaction. Therefore, the primary access should be to the series or 'block' of associated records. Access to an individual document is a secondary route, only justified in terms of the overheads which it involves on the basis of strategic business need and the careful structuring outlined in the first section of this chapter. This is a factor largely ignored so far by the vendors of computer systems software.

At the same time it has to be said that records managers have not been noticeably adept at information retrieval issues. Undoubtedly for the future this is going to be an area of increasing importance.

A first requirement will be to establish basic classification systems. The logical way to do this is to use the functional analysis method and to assign codes to each function, activity and process. The individual transactions (which may be separate documents) are then simply numbered serially (Fig. 7.6). Where existing classifications have to be adapted, it may be necessary to add a further subdivision to integrate any existing reference (see Fig. 7.7) where the term 'application' has been used for this. Since it is impossible to have, for example, a file at the purely functional level, the problem of general classification is eliminated. More importantly, the use of functional analysis relates to records directly to the information structure and strategy already discussed, once again illustrating how important this is for getting the records management design correct.

FUNCTION	ACTIVITY	PROCESS	TRANSACTION
Marketing	Publicity	Advertising	Newspaper ads
			TV ads
			Radio ads

Fig. 7.6:   The FAPT system. (*Source*: Strategic Information Management.)

It is important to realise that a classification scheme is the creation of the information 'boxes' into which records can be fitted. It does not provide, of itself, a way of knowing what is in the 'boxes'. This can only be done by individual inventory at the transactional level. Whether such an inventory is needed is a management decision related to the strategic significance of the information being inventoried.

Figure 7.7 also illustrates the division of responsibility between corporate records management and the local records system. This

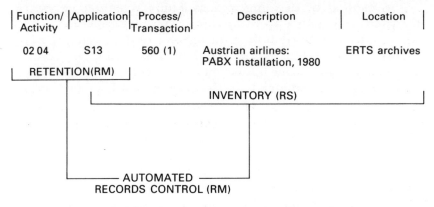

Fig. 7.7:   Developing retrieval and control.
(*Source*: Strategic Information Management.)

is vital in a large organisation, since it is impossible to establish transactional codes and references from the centre and the operators of the records must be left as free as possible to reference them in a way relevant to their work, provided the essential corporate needs for good management are met. In this connection, the role of the Automated Record Control System is seen as bringing together the retention system, which must be corporately monitored, and the inventory which, as we have seen, is a local matter.

This brings us to the question of retention. It has already been established in Chapter 4 that the setting up of an effective retention programme is a major benefit of a records management system. These benefits are not in any way lessened by the introduction of automation. It is sometimes strangely assumed that because the capacity of, for example, optical disk, is so great, data can be shovelled on to it without any concern for its ultimate retention. The fact is that this is an expensive and unwise approach, likely to produce in a few years the same kind of problems organisations now experience with uncontrolled hard copy records. Uncontrolled data is already a time-bomb ticking away in apparently highly effective modern computer systems. Opposing forces are at work here. On the one hand is the need to limit data to what is really usable and relevant, and on the other, an increasing tendency for law and regulation to demand that specific retention periods be assigned and that those already legally required should be extended. With certain classes of records now requiring at least thirty-year retention, the need to apply automation with the maximum strategic awareness is becoming acute.

The method of deciding and assigning retention periods is discussed in Chapter 4. Here the concern is with the methods which will need to be applied in the future. Some of these can indeed be undertaken now but as yet the inter-relationship of records management with other information management disciplines has not proceeded far enough to enable us to establish a total routine. In the traditional situation records analysis has played the key role. In the future a more integrated approach will be needed and the various steps are likely to be something like this:

1. Establishing the business areas of which an organisation is made up, i.e. the operational relationship rather than the organisation chart hierarchy.
2. Analysing the business areas into their respective activities and processes.
3. Determining the key things about which each of these areas needs to have information ('entities').
4. Analysing the inputs and outputs of each activity or process to discover which of them are in fact records, which external sources, which value-added data, etc.
5. Plotting the information so ascertained on to charts, tables and matrices to provide a graphic means of expressing the records structure of an organisation which also relates it to the total information resource picture.

It then becomes possible to concentrate on the records management issues *per se* by:

(a) analysing records in series;
(b) providing a checklist of records which are candidates for databases;
(c) applying functional codes; and
(d) evaluating for retention, security, etc.

It will also be possible to determine what groups of records belong together in the same system, what means of access are required, and using the functional analysis and entity lists, the referencing and indexing needs can be determined. This approach to information retrieval from records will be of major significance since it is important to recognise that current retrieval methods, especially indexing principles, are derived from library methods and the indexing of textual material. This is often quite inappropriate for records but little work to date has really been done on producing records-orientated indexing methods.

Restructuring, classification and indexing are significant steps, indeed perhaps nodal points, in the migration between present records systems and those of the future. This can be illustrated by Fig. 7.8 which demonstrates that the standard present-day method of filing records for retrieval under basically subject–type headings needs to be changed by the application of functional classification to enable records systems to be structured around the business areas of an organisation. However, the overhead in development time, plus some technical problems, is likely to mean that a proportion of existing records will have to stay in older systems. This is where the Automated Records Control System has an integrating role to play and can also be seen as a pathway to office automation.

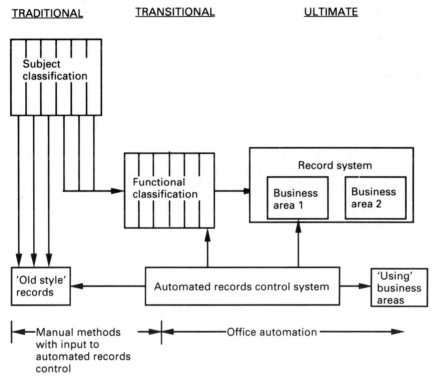

Fig. 7.8: Migration path of record systems.
(Source: Strategic Information Management.)

The automation of records management

The future of this subject seems to fall into two parts:

1. The automation of information about records in order to provide effective management decision-making and control systems.

2.   The automation of the process of records system design itself.

The first of these has already been undertaken to a limited extent, although not many operational systems fully address it, even now.[13] There are of course many applications of (usually) packaged software to the task of producing lists and indexes of records[14] but this is not what we are concerned with here. What is required is an automated system of establishing control over the physical record for management purposes rather than information retrieval. If we adopt the approach of the Anthony Triangle to the design of records management programmes (Fig. 7.9), the automated records control system must be seen as the foundation stone of the whole edifice. However, this analogy needs modification since if we pursue the 'top-down' approach which is advocated earlier in this chapter, the design of an ARCS will probably be the last, or nearly the last, stage in the whole process.

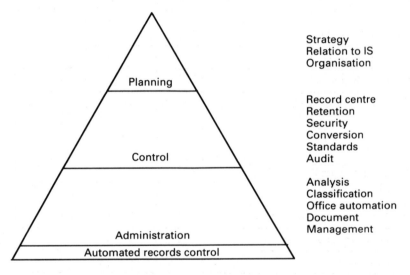

Fig. 7.9: Design pyramid based on the Anthony Triangle.
(*Source*: Strategic Information Management.)

The normal procedures for database design should be applied which means that the following steps have to be undertaken:

1.   Identify the activities which will create, modify, use, delete, access, etc., data in the system.
2.   Identify the data items (entities) which each of the above will require to function effectively.
3.   Matrix the activities and entities (Fig. 7.10).

4. Schedule the data requirements by activity.
5. Prepare a field definition specification (Fig. 7.11).
6. List the facilities which are required, notably the conditions and frequency of access for particular fields, display and print parameters and the primary access keys, i.e. the data items which are the main points of entry for any set. Thus date might be the primary key to data concerning the transfer of records to a record centre.
7. Specify the security requirements, i.e. which fields are un-amendable, amendable only on authorisation, accessible to limited user groups, etc.

Field No.	Entity / Activity	Inventory	Analysis	Assessment	Transfer	Storage	Disposal	Monitoring	User access
1	Organisational unit	C	U		U	U		U	
2	Function code	C	U					U/M	U
3	Application code	C	U						U
4	Process code	C	U						U
5	Item/series description	C	U/M						U
6	Item/series dates	C	U/M						U
7	Location	C	U						U
8	Current reference	C	U						U
9	Identifier		C	U			U	U	
10	Assigned series description		C				U	U	
11	Assigned series dates		C				U	U	
12	Quantity/form		C	U		U		U	
13	Medium		C			U		U	
14	Arrangement		C						U
15	Finding aids		C						U
16	Usage/access		C						U

Fig. 7.10:   An entity/activity matrix.
(*Source*: Strategic Information Management.)

If the database is to be fully relational a data model may also be needed. In addition there is value in preparing a schedule setting out the levels of document description to which each data item is

Field No.	Name	Source	Type	Length	Status	Validation, etc.
1	Oganisational unit	List	Alpha	Variable	M	Against list
2	Function code	List	Alpha/Numeric	6	M	Against list
3	Application code	Inventory	Alpha/Numeric	Variable	0	None
4	Process code	Inventory	Alpha/Numeric	Variable	0	None
5	Item/Series decription	Inventory	Free Text	Variable	M	Exsistence of text
6	Item/Series dates	Inventory	Numeric	Variable	M	Full year (1985) year/month (1985/12) range (1984-1991) open (1985-) intermittent (1985, 1988) year/day (1986/306)
7	Location	Inventory	Alpha/Numeric	Variable	M	Exsistence of entry
8	Current reference	Inventory	Alpha/Numeric	Variable	0	None
9	Identifier	Series	Integer	3	M	Check for uniqueness against field 1

Fig. 7.11:   Data field description.
(*Source*: Strategic Information Management.)

relevant (Fig. 7.12). At this stage the specification is ready for handing over to the technical design team.

The second type of records management automation, that of the records system design, raises much more intriguing possibilities and complications. Such an outcome is the natural corollary of adopting a strategic and structured approach. Already in the computer field the use of this approach has given rise to a number of products now designated as CASE tools (computer assisted systems engineering). It is possible to envisage the production of software which would take the results of the initial analysis of functions, information needs, inputs, outputs and produce full schedules of filing codes, retention assessments and even specify which records should be where. The main inhibition on this at the moment is the interface between the specification of standards, criteria, and technical requirements and non-automated records. Such records will exist for a long time to come but the problem is being largely ignored by the designers in the belief that it is not significant. In reality, it may well prove to be the crucial factor in whether organisations can really automate their records effectively. Given a solution to this problem, the day may come when the records manager can design a full scale system at a keyboard by accessing the analytical data stored in the information strategy database.

Undoubtedly records management is a significant and challenging tool for helping to take organisations into the next century.

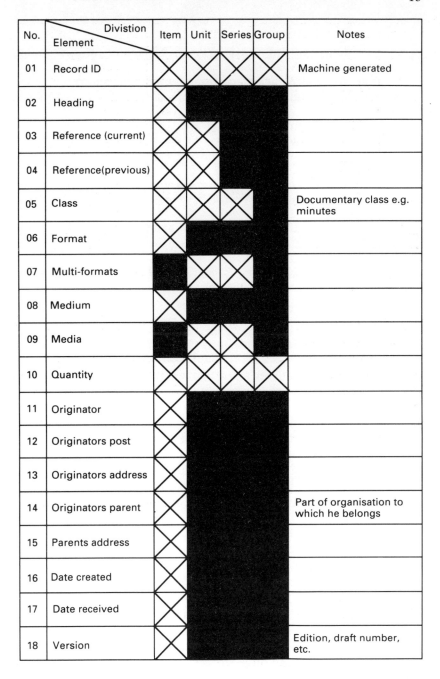

No.	Element / Division	Item	Unit	Series	Group	Notes
01	Record ID	X	X	X	X	Machine generated
02	Heading	X				
03	Reference (current)	X	X			
04	Reference(previous)	X	X			
05	Class	X	X	X		Documentary class e.g. minutes
06	Format	X				
07	Multi-formats		X	X		
08	Medium	X				
09	Media		X	X		
10	Quantity	X	X	X	X	
11	Originator	X				
12	Originators post	X				
13	Originators address	X				
14	Originators parent	X				Part of organisation to which he belongs
15	Parents address	X				
16	Date created	X				
17	Date received	X				
18	Version	X				Edition, draft number, etc.

Fig. 7.12: Schedule of records management and data elements.
(*Source*: James Martin Associates.)

Notes

1. Emmet J. Leahy and Christopher A. Cameron, *Modern Records Management*, New York, 1965.
   William Benedon, *Records Management*, Los Angeles, 1969.
2. T. R. Schellenberg, *Modern Archives: Principles and Techniques*, Chicago, 1956.
3. For example, Yourden, LBMS, Tetrarch, Information Engineering.
4. The classic text on critical success factors is John F. Rockart, 'Chief executives define their own data needs', *Harvard Business Review*, March–April 1979, p.81.
5. See Carl Newton, 'Records management and business information systems', *Business Archives: Principles and Practice*, **55**, May 1988, especially pp.5–11.
6. Margaret L. Hedstrom, *Archives and Manuscripts: Machine-Readable Records*, Society of American Archivists Basic Manual Series, Chicago, 1984.
7. For example, James Martin, *Principles of Database Management*, Englewood Cliffs, New Jersey, 1976, especially Section IV.
8. James Martin, *An Information Systems Manifesto*, Englewood Cliffs, New Jersey, 1974, p. 95.
9. Peter Emmerson, 'Computer-generated records: some legal aspects', *Computer-Generated Records* (Seminar Proceedings), Society of Archivists, 1986, p. 32.
10. On the retention issue, see a short but stimulating contribution by Gilles Gauthier-Villars, 'New technologies for improved information systems and services', in *AGARD Conference Proceedings No. 385*, NATO, 1985, Section 9. For storage media, see A. M. Hendley, *The Archival Storage Potential of Microfilm, Magnetic Media and Optical Disk*, Hatfield: NRCd, 1983.
11. A conference presentation quoted in *Inform* (Institute of Information Scientists), July/August, 1988, p. 7.
12. See *Text Retrieval 86: Full Text Rules OA?*, Institute of Information Scientists, 1986 (though it must be said the question mark indicates some doubts).
13. For applications in government see *Information Technology in the Registry*, London: HMSO/CCTA, 1986.
14. See, for example, Rachel Bartle and Michael Cook, *Computer Applications in Archives: A Survey*, University of Liverpool (BLRDD Report 5749), 1983. Despite the title this includes records management applications in academic, government and commercial environments.

CHAPTER 8

THE PROBLEMS OF PARTICULAR ORGANISATIONS

Compiled by

CAREY MORAN

Records Manager, MEPC PLC

Introduction

Previous chapters have dealt with the general principles and practices of establishing and developing a records management programme. This chapter aims to cover the records management problems which are unique to companies, partnerships, universities, charities and local government and to apply those general principles to them.

Most principles of records management are the same, whatever type of institution is involved. However, organisations will also produce records which are specific to themselves, and develop individual approaches as the result of their own particular environment, influenced by the institution's own area of activity, by the rules under which it operates and by the people who are responsible for its running.

For a company this special group of records will be those concerning its responsibility towards its investors, the shareholders. A partnership works for a client who commissions them to act on his behalf. Universities run research and teaching programmes paid for by public money. A charity deals with donated money and must justify all money spent on its own administration. Local government exists to support its elected members in disbursing public funds and administering political instructions. The problems raised as a result of these areas are discussed below.

Companies

Nature of a company

Earlier chapters have established the need to be aware of the main legislation under which companies act and their legal, regulatory and financial obligations. There are some additional points worth making as to the nature of a company.

A company exists to make a profit for those who own it or have a stake in it. Profit will govern what happens in a company – how many and what type of staff are employed, the kind of equipment used, what is produced, how it is sold and where. A records management programme's best chance of establishment and survival in a company will be because of the promise of greater efficiency in retrieval, the freeing of office space, use of lower cost storage and the destruction of records as soon as legal restraints allow. Talk of establishing an archive to show the history and development of the company may be a beneficial by-product of a records management programme but it is low on the list of most companies' priorities in their quest for cost efficiency.

A company records management programme must also cope with the range of records produced. A multinational company may have interests ranging from a stud farm to an open cast mine to double glazing. While the principles of what is done with the records are generally the same, the programme must be detailed enough to cope with legislation which affects every area and have retention schedules which are specific to the records produced rather than so general as to be irrelevant.

A company is on constant display to its investors, the customers and governing bodies. A variety of organisations have the right of access to a company's affairs, for example the Inland Revenue, Customs and Excise, the Department of Industry, the Stock Exchange, Monopolies and Mergers Commission, shareholders, external auditors, EC Commissioners and external creditors. Failure to produce information when required, to be unable to show transactions and decisions in certain areas, particularly relating to the financial position of the company, may lead to punitive fines, the withdrawal of operating licences or being forced to go into liquidation. Efficient management of company records may help in producing the right information when it is required.

Legislation

Under the Companies Act 1985, a company is formed by incorporation and may be limited by shares, limited by guarantee, unlimited, or a public company. A memorandum must be lodged at Companies House stating the name of the company, where it is registered and its objects. With at least £100 share capital, two issued shares and the names of one director and one secretary, the company can begin to trade. It can range in size from two members to thousands and have an unlimited range of activities.

Apart from the size of a company and its sphere of business operation, the main differences between companies are those which are privately owned and those which are publicly quoted.

Public companies must have an authorised share capital of 50,000 shares. In order to be admitted to the Stock Exchange, the company must fulfil the requirements of the Stock Exchange Yellow Book, *Admission of Securities to Listing*. The Yellow Book and *The City Code on Takeovers and Mergers and The Rules Governing Substantial Acquisitions of Shares*, which is also issued by the Stock Exchange, detail the rules, additional to the Companies Act under which a quoted company is placed.

This book governs, in all areas, how a company must act in relation to its shareholders and the raising of capital by shares. It lays out the special responsibilities and obligations of the company. The principles are worth quoting in full:

The requirements set out seek to secure the confidence of investors in the conduct of the market by ensuring first that all applicants for listing are of a certain minimum size, have a record of trading of adequate duration under their present management and set out in formal listing particulars or equivalent offering documents sufficient information about their history, prospects and financial condition to form a reliable basis for market evaluation; secondly that all marketings of securities are conducted on a fair and open basis, allowing the public access wherever appropriate; and, finally, that investors are treated with proper consideration at all times by company boards, even though the public may only represent a minority of the shareholders.

Greater detail is required from a quoted company concerning its financial state so that investors are secure in their investment. Public companies are responsible to their shareholders to act in their best interests, to improve profits, to protect their investments from fraud and bad or corrupt management.

A company records management programme must cope with keeping detailed information required to fulfil the wide range of legislation while bearing in mind the emphasis constantly running through a company of cost and profitability in all areas.

Further reading on companies

Admission of Securities to Listing, the Council of the Stock Exchange, 1984.

The City Code on Takeovers and Mergers and the Rules of Governing

Substantial Acquisitions of Shares, the Council of the Stock Exchange, 1988.

Butterworths Company Law Guide, Butterworths, 1985.

Partnerships

The main difference between partnerships and companies in the retention of records lies in their being involved with clients on a personal level and from holding many documents that actually belong to the client and not themselves. This, of course, also happens in some companies, but not to such a great extent. Stemming from this is the partnership's liability for professional negligence and for the maintenance of confidentiality.

Legislation

Legislation affecting partnerships alone is still the Partnership Act 1890 with the Limited Partnership Act 1907 and occasional reference in various Companies Acts. There is no legal requirement in any of the legislation for records to be held for any particular length of time. Proper accounts have to be kept but at the end of the year, when agreed, they could theoretically be destroyed. For all such documents, therefore, the length of retention is governed by Inland Revenue and Customs and Excise requirements.

The main document of a partnership is its deed – although there is no legal necessity for such a document and there are misguided partnerships which do not have one. This document can be of vital importance in times of stress and it is suggested that originals of all such deeds are held throughout the life of the partnership like similar legal documents in other organisations. All partners should have their own signed copy which should be placed in a secure location.

The length of time records need to be held is covered in the main by the requirements of the Latent Damage Act 1986, the Companies Acts and the Limitation Act 1980 but also by others impinging on small sections. To hold everything for the maximum time that might be needed will ensure that every piece of paper is kept indefinitely. A commercial decision has to be made regarding what can be destroyed, microfilmed or held in its original form. This policy needs to be set down in writing by the partners but each appointment needs to be reviewed by a partner or senior member of staff who can weigh up all the considerations.

Retention of records

Ownership of records

The majority of decisions affecting retention of documents in a partnership hinge around commercial considerations and many of these are common to all professions. Most professional firms hold original documents of legal value for their clients. Solicitors hold wills, chartered secretaries hold statutory books and accountants hold trust instruments. These need to be held throughout the working life of the client as they are irreplaceable and major decisions can depend on their contents and provenance.

For the majority of documents the first fact that has to be decided is their ownership. Documents owned by a party other than the partnership may not be destroyed without the prior consent of the person to whom they belong. Should such documents be destroyed without permission, the partnership may be liable for any loss accruing. It is easy to think of examples of documents that can remain valuable for many years such as those relating to the purchase of a company or of a building. Copyright should not be confused with ownership, for the client may be forbidden to use a document for a purpose other than that for which it was intended but will still own it. As a good working principle, if a client has paid for a document, it is owned by that client. Examples of this would be audit reports bills of quantities and deeds. Drafts and copies as well as final documents are covered by this principle.

Documents prepared by the partnership for its own protection, such as letters to and from the client, would not normally be regarded as owned by the client and the same applies to diaries, time sheets and similar records. However, documents prepared by a third party and sent to the partnership are owned by the client.

Retention periods – trustees

Partnerships of many types become involved as trustees and, in that capacity, can have their conduct questioned by any future beneficiary. The minutes and records of the trust, therefore, should be held throughout the life of the trust as it is normally a practical impossibility to obtain a discharge from every possible interested person. An alternative is to cover the risk with insurance. If records are microfilmed, then the requirements laid down as in Chapter 5 are equally applicable to partnerships as to any other organisation.

Retention periods – construction industry

Different groups of professions have different problems and they therefore need to be considered separately. The construction industry partnerships of architects, engineers and surveyors are particularly affected by the Latent Damage Act 1986. The details of the Act are irrelevant to this subject but the periods of liability are of great importance. There are two cut-off points and a long stop period for negligent acts. The first cut-off point is a basic limitation period of six years from the point at which the damage was discovered. The long-stop is fifteen years after the negligent breach of duty.

The significance of the basic period and the discovery period is irrelevant to the retention of documents, because it must be supposed that a discovery could be made at any time and relevant documents ought to be held for fifteen years. This period should probably run from practical completion of the contract. As always, nothing is cut and dried. Under the Civil Liability (Contribution) Act 1978, a defendant who has had a judgment awarded against him in legal proceedings may recover a contribution from a third party who is partly to blame for the loss. This action may be commenced up to two years after judgment has been awarded against the defendant and, as it could take several years to come to trial in the first place, the length of potential liability is much greater than fifteen years. It is suggested, however, that this danger is in reality not great since the partnership will be well aware if proceedings are expected on any of their contracts and will know which documents need to be held. The remainder can be disposed of after fifteen years.

Most contracts entered into by the construction professions are not under seal and, therefore, liability runs under the Limitation Act for a period of six years from breach of contract. There is, however, a move to introduce contracts under seal which extends the period of liability to twelve years. There is also an increasing requirement for letters of warranty to be given to third parties and these are frequently requested to be under seal. The latter also normally includes a right for the third party to see any documents produced by the partnership. If for no other reason than the problems of document retention, the signing of contracts under seal should be resisted and the signing of warranties for third parties that are more onerous than the original contracts should be refused. It is wise for letters of warranty to be amended to allow sight of extant documents only.

The construction professions collect a vast quantity of drawings which are much more expensive to microfilm than ordinary documents. The originator may microfilm their copies but other partnerships can destroy theirs after the contract. Originators should be wary of microfilming drawings and destroying the originals unless fully discussed since they can never be brought back accurately to scale. The general rule should be that when the contract is completed and the final fee account has been paid, a short period of about six months should be allowed to pass and then the files should be divided into those for destruction and those for retention. The policy should be to keep or destroy complete files and, if a file is mixed, then it should be left.

Retention periods – accountants and financial advisers
The professional dealing with taxation affairs can probably, more readily than most, dispose of the majority of documents by returning them to the client with an adequate proviso regarding the necessity to hold them while the Inland Revenue has a right to review the case. The records for chargeable assets for capital gains purposes need to be kept during the life of the client and for a suitable time thereafter. This means that records have to be maintained for the purchase, conversion, improvement and sale of the asset and also for chargeable and exempt transfers.

As the Inland Revenue can go back over a very long period if it believes fraud has taken place, comparative schedules should be maintained for year by year tax returns. This removes the necessity of keeping the actual returns themselves.

The actual destruction of financial documents, even more than any others, needs to be done with care as confidential papers getting into the wrong hands can prove very embarrassing and indeed expensive. All such papers should therefore be shredded or pulped under supervision.

Retention periods – problem records
One of the main reasons for holding documents in partnerships is as a protection if sued. Professional indemnity insurers will always wish proper records of all transactions to be maintained and held for as long as possible. When preparing documents for destruction, therefore, it should always be asked whether they might be needed for this purpose. The answer does not only depend on the nature of the documents but also on the type and result of the appointment.

Some jobs cause problems throughout and they are always more likely to give rise to litigation. Indeed, by the time an appointment is completed, it will probably be known that legal action is possible. These jobs should have their documents treated with much more circumspection than more straightforward cases. There is good reason for seeing that the files are complete, making notes of any information missing, with contemporary details recorded and signed. The records should be well indexed and kept in a place where they are both accessible and secure from damage.

With other appointments it is certain aspects that give rise more readily to litigation than others. Design calculations produced by consulting engineers are an obvious example of this. Consideration needs to be given to this aspect when preparing files for destruction and the more sensitive elements should be treated in the same manner as documents for problem appointments.

Holding documents to provide a defence for a client can be a dangerous exercise as well as a costly one. It is always possible that the documents that have been carefully preserved actually prove the client to be liable. There is no kudos in holding documents for this purpose alone and they should be destroyed in line with normal policy.

To summarise, the special retention and destruction problems of the professions stem from the personal relationship with the client resulting in confidential documents being held that belong sometimes to the client and sometimes to the professional. However, it should be possible, through applying the techniques described in this book, to identify those categories of records which need to be retained.

Disposal of documents owned by clients

Disposing of documents owned by a client is always tricky. The easiest thing is to write a standard letter to the client requesting either that the document be returned to him or his signature on a disclaimer at the foot of the letter and its return. This produces two possible reactions other than the rare one of a signed and returned document. The first and most frequent reaction is no reply. This leaves the partnership in the difficult position of having acknowledged that it has the documents and that it realises it should not destroy them without permission. The second is a letter refusing permission to destroy and not accepting the return of the documents. The problems of the first possibility are exacerbated by the refusal of permission to destroy, and the remaining option of destroying the documents notwithstanding will alienate the client and possibly the client's friends and acquaintances.

A method sometimes used is an inertia instruction. The letter says that if a reply is not received within, say, seven days, the documents will be returned or destroyed. This is all very well for the return of documents, but it does not free the partnership from the legal liability of destroying documents without the express consent of the owner. It also sometimes elicits a prompt refusal which not only produces the same result as the previous method but also an even more upset client. The only sure method, other than to hold the documents indefinitely, is to return them with a polite covering letter. When documents are returned, the client should be warned of any liability incurred by their destruction.

Documents produced by a third party have been referred to already. Those in the ownership of the client are fairly few, being for such things as reports commissioned from other professions or receipts for disbursements made on behalf of the client. For the remainder it is perfectly acceptable to take the view that documents prepared for the client by a third party, of which a copy is sent to the partnership for some purpose, need not be held as it is the producer's responsibility to hold the document for the client. Requests are frequently made to all and sundry for copies of old documents and this merely reflects the fact that the originator's copy has been destroyed or mislaid.

Permanent retention of records

The construction professions in particular, the legal profession to a considerable extent and all professions to some degree, hold documents of historic value to future generations. One has only to consider the interest in the designs of Christopher Wren, legal documents from the Middle Ages, or accounts from feudal manors to see what is involved. It is also, of course, of particular value to the firm to have records from the past because it demonstrates its longevity and reputation. Very few firms have them, however, for it is difficult to know what will be of value, and costly to hold everything that might be.

If it is considered that documents of historic value are held, it is advisable to consult the county archivist who will arrange for a confidential inspection and provide advice on their future survival and including possibly their deposit at the County Record Office.

Universities

The nature of a university

Universities are among the most important institutions of modern society. A typical British university has a community of between ten and fifteen thousand people, and has an annual budget of around £40–70 million: this means that they are among the largest employers, comparable with large firms, but quite different in structure and aims.

It would be natural to apply the same methods of analysis to universities as to businesses or other organisations. However, much of the language of systems analysis is inappropriate to universities. They have no raw material or product in the tangible sense, and no clients as understood in business. Despite this, most universities interact strongly with their regions and with business and industrial firms, not only locally but internationally. The aim of the university is to extend and communicate knowledge, and the spread of interest and expertise available in universities as a body is as wide as all human experience.

A university is a collection of different interests, styles and pursuits. The large faculty units carry out research and teaching in broad subjects, such as chemistry, physics, mathematics and English. Within these subject areas, special units work at particular projects. Specialist training schools produce personnel for medicine, architecture, law, education and librarianship. Most of these reach out into the wider community through professional structures such as hospitals, professional associations, courts, schools and local authorities.

Within the university departments are the basic working units, and these have traditionally had a good deal of autonomy. Linking them is a structure of administration backed by common services such as a library, computing, finance, central student and staff services and machinery for policy and decision-making.

All these activities result in the collection and dissemination of information and records. The university itself has channels for these, and at present they are in the process of being computerised, with electronic mail, recording systems and linked databases. The world's universities are already linked in a system of communication networks: the British one is JANET (Joint Academic Network), which has gateways to European and American networks. Electronic communication is already common and several central university co-ordinating bodies maintain electronic directories and/or billboards.

Legislation

British universities are technically autonomous, under their Royal charters. The governing body is usually a formal assembly. Financial affairs are dealt with by Council, whose membership is often reinforced by senior business people. Academic concerns are dealt with by Senate, consisting of academic members. These two bodies meet regularly (at least three times a year each) in an annual cycle, and have a large number of committees. Faculty boards co-ordinate broad subject areas. Schools and departments are run by boards, of which all staff involved are usually members. Overall, a high proportion of staff and students are involved in these bodies.

The principal officer, the Vice-Chancellor, is an academic in background, and is in overall charge of both academic and financial development. Below him in the central administration, there are chief officers with departments: the Registrar or Secretary (in effect a chief executive), finance, building and personnel directors. Faculties have an equivalent structure, headed by Deans, and with professional administrators.

University income comes mainly from government, and the Auditor General has an overall power of inspection of records. Other sources of income are from endowments, grants from external bodies and from the product of research or consultancy work; student fees are also an important source.

Data protection of course applies, and the Act has had some important effects in the university field. The traditionally secret records of marks awarded to students have now been open since 1988. There will undoubtedly be further changes in record confidentiality and in the attitudes of staff towards them.

Records created by universities

Records could be controlled by statutes and ordinances issued under the terms of each university's charter, but this is rarely done. It is often difficult to distinguish official from private records. The principal officers are always academics, who have research and other interests (and hence documents) dealing with specialist areas. For example, the Dean of a faculty of medicine will maintain records on university development policy, on research progress in the faculty's medical specialty, on external funding and on the activities of the professional group. Deans of faculties and heads of department are customarily appointed for short terms in rotation among the academic staff, so that each senior member will tend to have records of all of these kinds.

Within the university, the main accumulations of records arise from the committee system and its offshoots, the student recording system, staff records, financial administration, fabric maintenance and research. There are committees, boards and working parties at every level. The main ones are serviced by professional administrators who hold the official record centrally and circulate copies widely. Departmental committees are serviced by one of their own members and there is no certainty that their records will be kept, distributed or written up to a definite standard.

The main student record is kept centrally. This records the student's progress through the university and will have to be kept for current reference indefinitely. Requests for degree certificates can be received up to sixty years after graduation, sometimes beyond. Other records are generated on the same individual students, in the faculties and in the departments, and these can often have significant variations from the central record.

Staff and financial records broadly resemble those in other institutions, except for the possibility that they will document important new developments of great future significance. A particular feature is the annual assessment of individual members of staff, which generates much confidential paperwork.

The records of fabric maintenance may often have special importance. The university's own buildings are likely to include at least some with special significance and value. In other cases the record of the site may have special importance for the history of the local community. Plans and development records may exist in considerable quantity.

University records demonstrate some other special features. Confidentiality is unusually important. Some areas of research or activity are very sensitive. For example, most universities have laboratory animals whose welfare attracts violent public attention. These animals also have to be dealt with within an elaborate code of ethics, which demands careful records. Health and safety is complex, involving radioactive and chemical materials, and often dangerous experiments. A high proportion of the records generated contain references to, and judgements on, individuals. The individuals concerned may be famous or outstanding, or potentially so. Research records often deal with industrial innovations and new patents. Confidential disposal of records demands much care.

Records management in the university

It must be clear from this brief survey that a university is a very complex institution in which the creation and exploitation of records is likely to be particularly important.

Because of the special nature of many of these records, a high proportion of university records cannot be routinely disposed of under retention schedules, but have to be reviewed. The filing systems of university officers or of individuals contain copies of administrative records, and often policy papers concerning special-ist or research projects also. Routine departmental files may contain contract documents relating to externally financed research, or the raw data of similar research in the past.

Research documentation may be linked to physical installations, or to pieces of scientific equipment, and it may be necessary to appraise and preserve both in association with each other.

Appraisal is likely to be particularly difficult where highly specialised work, especially perhaps work in the hard sciences, is involved.

For these reasons, retention schedules covering university records are difficult to construct. Few exist at present and there seems to be little impetus towards sharing the results of this type of work (Bott and Edwards, 1978). More work has been done in the USA than in Britain: some results have been published by the Society of American Archivists (Saffady, 1979).

Records management within the university usually suffers from the informal traditions of financial management. During 1988/9 a new system of financial management is being introduced to most British universities, in which funds and accounting responsibility are devolved from the centre to the departments. This will mean a dispersal of records, but the change is not likely to be so radical as to involve strict accountability for premises and accommodation. In the absence of a notional rent for office space, it is difficult for records managers to cost their service, especially since accommodation is frequently in older, not fully adapted buildings.

In this atmosphere it is difficult to make a case for investing in warehousing for the records centre. Campuses are usually extensive and scattered and in many (but not all) cases, away from high-cost city centres. The tradition of departmental autonomy militates against centralised services, including records management. The tradition of delegating concern for historical archives to the library also tends to make records management difficult. It is remarkable that despite these problems several universities have made important progress in managing their records and developing records management as an aspect of the management sciences.

There is one interesting additional feature. Universities do regard the record of their own personnel and activities as having a special interest for the future, and can often be persuaded to preserve material on this account: it is an appraisal principle. The interest of large numbers of people is involved, and it would be a pity to discourage this aspect of university life.

Conclusion

Universities are complex institutions in which recording systems are particularly important. They contain documentation on a wide range of subjects, including highly specialised ones, and ones which bear upon important aspects of society. The universities also employ and train a high proportion of those individuals who use archive and record material professionally. Despite these features, and despite the work achieved in several universities in Britain and elsewhere, there are no established standards. It is not publicly established that research findings should be recorded systematic- ally, nor that financial provision should be made for this in research funding. It is not a standard that there should be a records management system, or provision for one in the administrative structure. Senior management has not yet provided a system which responds to the cost benefits of good records management.

The Society of Archivists (acting initially through its Specialist Repositories Group) and the Standing Conference of National and University Libraries (SCONUL) have set up a joint working party on university records and their management. This body has investigated the situation during 1987/8 and intends to issue a report, including case studies, during 1989 (Methven, 1988).

Further reading on universities

Allan, A. R., *Para-educational Forces: A Survey of Inter- and Supra-university Bodies and their Records*, in the course of publication by the Society of Archivists, Specialist Repositories Group, 1989.

Bott, M. and Edwards, J. A., *Records Management in British Universities: A Survey with some Suggestions*, University of Reading, 1978.

Methven, P.C. convenes the working party 1988; College Archives, King's College, London.

Saffady, W., 'A university archives and records management program: some operational guidelines', in *College and University Archives: Selected Readings*, Society of American Archivists, Chicago, 1979, pp. 97–103.

Schmidt, W. F. and Wilson S. J., 'A practical approach to university records management', *ibid.*, pp. 104–18.

Charities

The nature of a charity

Charities are very much in the news at this time, and public and political interest in them has probably never been stronger. It is right that this should be so, in view of their standing, nationally and internationally, and the growth in their number and the present scale of their financial activities.

This interest has given rise to several government reports, such as that of the National Audit Office, and most comprehensively, the scrutiny by a special Home Office Committee under Sir Philip

Woodfield, covering the effectiveness of the existing system of supervision. Its main recommendations include a strengthening of this side of the work of the Charity Commission, a computerised register, and improved accounting standards; major new legislation, the first since the Charities Act 1960, is obviously in the offing. Sound records management therefore has a crucial place in the quest for cost-effectiveness and efficiency. Charities, especially those dependent upon public support, will wish to be, and be seen to be, determined in this endeavour.

Legislation

The administration and records management will depend to a great extent upon how the charity is legally constituted. The most common forms are:

(a) Trust Deed (the traditional form);
(b) Company (usually one limited by Guarantee);
(c) Unincorporated Association; and
(d) Royal Charter.

Obviously the Company registration will involve the heaviest statutory obligations, such as an AGM, annual returns and a competent professional level of record-keeping. Charities may also form trading subsidiary companies which pass their profits to the charity by means of a variable deed of covenant.

Whatever the legal structure, accurate record-keeping will cover the trustees' term of office, appointment and retirement; ages (if retirement at a certain age is mandatory); delegation (specific power must be given); committees (*ad hoc* and permanent) and their terms of reference; declaration of interests (so that any possible conflict may be foreseen). Except where the charity is incorporated (perhaps by company under guarantee), the trustees have ultimate responsibility for charity funds and in certain circumstances could be personally liable.

Official Custodian for Charities

The services of the Official Custodian for Charities are designed to ease the burden of paper work for charities, providing without charge a registration service, payment of gross income, notification of redemptions and other events requiring action by trustees. The Custodian does not give investment advice. The Woodfield Committee has recommended that the functions of the Custodian should be curtailed.

Property may also be registered in the name of the Official Custodian to avoid having to make transfers upon a change in trusteeship and as a safeguard against fraud.

Legal obligations

Accounting

The Accounting Standards Committee has published a recommended practice for charities, which goes well beyond the somewhat basic requirements of the Charities Act 1960. The main recommendations are:

to provide information on the history and constitution of the charity in the annual report; to include an Income and Expenditure Account, on an accruals, rather than a receipts and payments basis, and including gains and losses on investments; give details of the various funds of the charity including any special purpose or designated funds, explain exceptional items in detail; ensure that expenditure on fixed assets should be capitalised and depreciated at appropriate rates, the results of special ventures should include the full figures of income and expenses, not merely the net result.

Taxation

Taxation, in the main, is conspicuous by its absence from the world of charities. The principal concern of trustees and administrators is to ensure that full advantage is gained from this freedom. Appeal literature aimed at selected potential donors should stress the exemption, without restriction as to the amount, from Inheritance Tax. Many charities derive a large part of their regular income from legacies and bequests.

Any gains on disposal of an asset to a charity are not chargeable to Capital Gains Tax. Here again, the fund-raising potential is obvious. An indisputable record should be kept to prove that any donated asset which has accumulated a liability to Capital Gains Tax in the hands of the donor, has actually passed to the charity before disposal. The profits on disposal of property or investments by the charity likewise do not attract Capital Gains Tax, provided proceeds are applied for its charitable purposes.

Charities may arrange matters so as to make full use of exemption from Income Tax. Interest and dividends are paid gross if investments are registered through the Official Custodian for Charities or invested in special Exempt Unit Trusts. Deposit accounts with the Charities Deposit Fund are automatically paid gross and arrangements may be made with banks and building societies to avoid deduction of Income Tax from interest. Much record-keeping and time may be saved in these ways. Companies formed by charities for trading purposes may convenant their profits to the charity by means of a variable Deed of Covenant. (Deeds of Covenant in general are dealt with under 'Fund-Raising'.)

The measures introduced by the Finance Act 1986, intended to avoid abuse of charity status, made a distinction between qualifying and non-qualifying expenditure of a charity. These areas need not concern the majority of charities, which raise their income by way of donations.

Voluntary payments by a charity to individuals or other charitable institutions in furthering its objects (such as relief of need, hardship and distress) are not taxable. They are also disregarded from the calculation of benefits such as Housing and Income Support up to £5 per week if regularly paid; higher occasional lump sum payments are also disregarded.

Value Added Tax is an exception to the general rule of charity exemption in that the tax attaches to particular types of transactions and is concerned less with the organisation or individual transacting the business. A charity must register for VAT if its annual 'taxable supplies' exceed £21,300. There is specific relief for donated medical equipment and aids for the handicapped.

Investment

Trustees have a duty to take advice and to manage investments prudently. Unless the constitution specifically allows wider powers, the trustees are bound by the Trustees Investments Act 1961, under which, if they wish to put money into equities, the fund must be divided; 50 per cent minimum into Narrower Range (mainly gilts, deposits and debentures) and up to 50 per cent into Wider Range (mainly ordinary shares and unit trusts).

The Charities Act 1960 allows investment in common investment funds so that charities may benefit from economies of scale and reduced risks by pooling of funds. The Charities Official Investment Fund, the most popular vehicle for such pooling, may operate in both the Narrower and Wider Ranges. There are also reputable non-official common funds.

Accounting records should be adequate to ensure compliance with the Trustees Investments Act or other specific powers and facilitate conformity with the statement of accounting practice.

Many charities seek to pursue an ethical investment policy to ensure that they are not supporting business activities which conflict with their aims or which they may consider morally unacceptable. On the positive side, they may wish to help the development of enterprises with which they are in sympathy. Either way, these policies call for constant vigilance backed by up-to-date information upon companies in which there may be indirect, as well as direct, investment.

Insurance

Trustees are obliged to protect the charity's assets to their full value by insurance and to cover for Public Liability and Employers' Liability where appropriate. They should also be satisfied that landlords, contractors and professional advisers have covered fully any risks affecting the charity. Records should be adequate to keep cover up to date.

Property

Most charities occupy property and some older ones may have a considerable investment in it as part of their permanent endowment. In the simplest case, where a charity is the freeholder and occupier, its property should be part of a comprehensive schedule of assets, and the record should include plans and drawings, costs of acquisitions and additions, rateable value (and any Charity Reliefs), insurance cover, etc.

Where the charity is either a landlord or a tenant, the record would include the main features of the lease or leases, the date entered into, its terms, the rent (with due dates), rent reviews, repairs and improvements (and by whom made), assignments/sub-lettings, periods of vacancy insurance cover, special listing under the Town and Country Planning Act 1948 (if any), service charges and a plan of the exact demise. A full maintenance manual is essential, with plans including services (on a practical scale), inspection dates, work done, contractors, surveyors/architects, health and safety and insurance inspections, and emergency telephone numbers for electricity, gas, drainage, fire hydrants, etc.

Rates

Property in charitable occupation and used for charitable purposes is granted statutory relief of 50 per cent by the Local Authority, which may grant discretionary relief up to a further 50 per cent in addition. It is worth keeping a record of the attitude (which may change from time to time) of various local authorities to discretionary relief and take this into account when considering the location of charity headquarters. Charities with a strong local connection are sometimes favoured in this respect.

It is proposed, from April 1990, to introduce a universal rate poundage to be known as the National Non-Domestic Rate. This rate will be set by the government and not by local authorities. At the same time there is to be a general rating revaluation, the first since 1973. Appeals against the revaluation will be subject to new tighter procedures. It is believed that a system of charity relief similar to the existing one will operate but charities should take care that questionnaires, appeals and applications for relief are dealt with in good time.

Special legislation applies to charity shops, which is intended to favour shops selling mainly donated goods as opposed to those which are outlets for goods bought commercially. This may also be subject to changes.

There is no relief for charities from water and sewerage charges, but it is worth keeping test records of water consumption to see if there is any advantage in having the supplies metered.

Fund-raising

Concern has been expressed at some of the methods by which money is raised for charity. Reputable charities will ensure that their rules, procedures and record-keeping are exemplary. Many of the better-known charities will have experienced voluntary regional helpers to look after this important side of their work, so that enthusiasm is balanced by practical controls and prudence. Particular attention is needed with regard to competitions, lotteries, sponsored events, street and house-to-house collections, media block-busters, telephone appeals, unattended collection boxes, professional fund-raising, and above all, joint enterprises. The latter area is a particularly difficult one for charities, who may not be aware until after the event that their names are being used. Strict accounting and record-keeping should be insisted upon.

Deeds of covenant

Covenants have been a mainstay of charities for many years, the legal commitment by the covenant giving the charity a reliable income during the term. Covenant administration requires an efficient system of record-keeping which can be labour-intensive. Several computer-based agencies such as the Charities Aid Foundation will undertake on a fee basis the tax recovery side. For covenanted payments below £175 net per annum the Revenue Claims Office may repay tax after the first year without production of a signed tax certificate.

A lump sum donation from a taxpayer may be turned into a 'deposited' covenant with the advantage of tax repayment added to the amount given. Income Tax repayment claims must be submitted within six years of the end of the year to which they relate.

Give as you earn

The payroll deduction scheme was introduced in the Finance Act 1986. From 6 April 1988 an employer may, at the request of an employee, deduct up to £240 annually from taxable pay and transfer it through an approved agency, such as the Charities Aid Foundation, to the charity or charities chosen by the employee. Schemes must have Inland Revenue approval. The potential income for charities is considerable, although the indications are that employees and employers have not so far been over-eager to embark upon this rather cumbersome system.

The Data Protection Act 1984

Charities holding information in computer form on individuals, such as beneficiaries of the charity, must register under this Act with the Data Protection Registrar. If such information is confined to manual record systems there is no need to register; even in such cases, information on individuals may occasionally be put on a word processor for the use of committees. There are limited exceptions covering individual medical records and for government departments, local authorities and voluntary organisations in respect of data held in connection with social work. If in any doubt, a charity should register.

Staff

Most charities are employers and, as such, incur legal obligations. Many will wish to pursue enlightened personnel policies, sensitive to the needs of employees who may be very highly motivated, and may see their work as a vocation. The more senior members of staff may be influential in policy matters within the charity. Where voluntary workers are engaged, a meticulous record should be kept of their contribution to further such goodwill, so that they are regarded as an integral part of the organisation.

Retention periods

Charities must keep the following documents throughout their existence:

(a) original trust deeds with any amendments;
(b) Charity Commissioners orders, especially those varying the trust;
(c) deeds of appointment and retirement of trustees, and death certificates of trustees who die in office;
(d) signed accounts; and
(e) minute books.

Accounts records should be kept for seven years (S32(2) Charities Act 1960) as well as those for payroll, income tax and VAT.

Archives
Charities came into being to meet particular needs and they have an important place in social and economic history. If day-to-day demands allow, a charity should seek to preserve archival material.

Local government

The nature of local government

Local government bodies consist of county councils, district and borough councils and metropolitan and London borough councils – the 'principal councils' which the Local Government Act 1972 (as amended by the Local Government Act 1986) charged with making 'proper arrangements' for their records. It is this imprecise phrase which has been used to justify the practice of records management by local authorities in England and Wales. These are also the councils which are entitled to exercise archive powers and it is probably no exaggeration to say that all the records management services worthy of the name in local government operate from within an archive service.

While the structure of local authorities has a considerable impact on their records management services, the other major influence lies in their business. The most significant difference between a local authority and a commercial organisation is that while one provides services to the public out of public funds, the other sells goods or services in an attempt to make a profit for its investors. In the process of discharging these roles the bodies resemble one another in many respects. Both may hold property, enter into contracts, employ staff, borrow and invest funds, pay and collect debts. These activities will produce similar records in both, subject for their retention to the same range of legislation and case-law on employment, limitation of actions, health and safety and so on. But in the delivery of services the authority is accountable to the public and is subject to the control of its elected representatives. It is funded from an annual budget, compounded of rate income supplemented by government grants, most notably the see-sawing rate support grant. The budget may not be exceeded yet must be spent each year if the following year's allocation is not to be prejudiced.

Because of public funding, a local council is obliged to maintain and to make available for its ratepayers a much wider range of records than is accessible to the shareholders in a commercial concern. Rating records are subject to inspection, while estimates, summaries of accounts and a report are published annually. Many of the local authority's tasks are undertaken in order to safeguard enduring public rights or to regulate local businesses and other organisations in the public interest. Registers and other records of these processes are numerous and in many cases long-term administrative retention shades into permanent archival preservation.

The formal proceedings of a council are similarly subject to scrutiny by the ratepayers and their informational content has been enhanced by the Local Government (Access to Information) Act 1985, a measure which reinforces the doctrine of public accountability. It insists on the disclosure, not only of the signed minutes of and reports to the council and its committees, but also of the background papers which substantiate the reports' opinions and proposals. It embodies the new spirit of openness urged on local government for the benefit of both the ratepayer and the 'customer' of its services. The doctrine is a stimulus to the efficient management of current and semi-current records and it may serve to shorten the perspective for archival review. If decisions are made public almost as soon as they are taken, the standard thirty-year public access restriction, which is common to many local archive services and reflected in the time-scale of review periods, may need reassessment.

History of records management in local government

The present situation stems from a tradition of local authority record-keeping which stretches back to the nineteenth century or even beyond, a tradition which expresses itself in well-developed filing and recording practices, administratively conservative but with a judicious respect for the need to document actions and decisions both for current business and for posterity. The clerk of the council (succeeded by the county, district or borough secretary in 1974) was the mainspring of this tradition and it was generally to his department that the first archivists were appointed in the mid-twentieth century. It was this background which bred the embryonic records management practice of offering time-expired records to the archivist for appraisal.

Once established, the records management service was likely to be a relatively autonomous unit; the records manager at its head, though answerable to the principal archivist, would usually be responsible for appraisal decisions. Local authority records managers are usually trained archivists, often with experience of work in the archive services section of a local records office; they may have responsibilities beyond the management of the pre-archival records of their own authorities. Historical factors account for many of the significant differences between the public and the private sector. The service is seldom introduced in a local council as a result of managerial initiative. Corporate management came late to local government and has not succeeded in stifling strong departmental identities. It is unusual for records to be viewed as a corporate information resource; vital records policies are rare.

Departmental independence may also make the achievement of corporate retention policies for record classes, which are common to more than one department, a difficult undertaking. Moreover, because there is none of the commercial organisation's concern for profitability, the approach to disposal tends to be less hard-nosed and aggressive and hence, perhaps, less cost-effective, than that of the private company. Cost savings may have priority over increases in efficiency and records control may remain underdeveloped and underpromoted by management. Retention decisions, administrative and archival, may be tinged with conservatism and the historical outlook.

The diversity of departmental 'cultures' within a local council is paralleled by the diversity of the records management services in local government as a whole. Indeed it must be remembered that the councils of some counties and many districts and boroughs do not lay claim to any such services. While some programmes exercise control over non-current records which remain in the administrators' storerooms, others incorporate fully developed records centres; some cater for the records of a few departments only, others for those of the whole organisation.

Retention policies

Only in the area of retention policies have tentative attempts at collaboration and conformity been made. Recently, under the aegis of the Records Management Group of the Society of Archivists, colleagues from different authorities have begun to identify record classes on a departmental basis and to try to establish guidelines for their retention. Their conclusions and some of the problems confronting them are to be found in the reports on the retention and management of social services and education records. The detail contained in these reports makes them suitable as an introduction to the subject of local government records management as a whole.

Though the public duty of proper retention of records is a solemn one, the formal, duly ratified, disposal schedule may be granted less prominence in the local government context. Both the daily conduct of business and strategic proposals are subject to regulation through inspection and audit, through requests for information and through the formal public inquiry. Local government functions have their basis in statutes, many of which specify the maintenance, though seldom the retention, of series of records. The volume of legislation, giving rise to the creation, transmogrification or termination of record classes, means that retention policies must be kept constantly under review.

The policy-making role of the council, as the local instrument of public control, also has its impact on the records. Elected for four years at a time, it may be incapable of evolving long-term strategies or consistent policies, especially when there are changes in its political balance or fluctuations in the sums of money available. The changing records produced by this process must be managed effectively; the policy changes to which they bear witness must be documented both for precedent and for future research.

Although routine housekeeping records are the same as those in commercial organisations, records relating to the provision of services are to be found in the public sector. Some of these services – road-building, fire-fighting, maintenance of public parks and consumer protection, for example – are provided for the community at large, while others – such as schools, old people's homes and council housing – are directed at certain sectors only. In the course of providing and establishing entitlement to these latter services in particular, the local authority amasses an immense quantity of information about the inhabitants of its area. The maintenance of personal, often confidential, data of this kind, which is usually tangential to the proper discharge of its duties, is one of the factors which differentiates the local authority most sharply from the average trading organisation. Examples are to be found in the case files on the educational and psychological welfare of school-children and on the financial circumstances of applicants for houses or for student grants, as well as in economic planning surveys of local firms. Many of these records need substantial administrative retention, both to prove that the local authority has acted in the public interest and, often, to provide a source of information to the client.

The judgement by which a commercial company decides to reduce a statutory retention period, accepting the financial risks of premature destruction, is not available to the public body. Yet there is a growing tendency (expressed in the Data Protection Act 1984) for records containing personally sensitive information to be destroyed as soon as possible after their operational life is over. The local government records management section, while conscious of being a repository of other people's secrets, is equally conscious of the twofold archival potential of these classes of particular instance papers, illuminating as they do both the authority's delivery of services and the wider community in which it operates. The records manager must try to resolve this tension in order to safeguard the permanent preservation of such records.

In highlighting the points of difference between the local authority and the commercial organisation, this section has deliberately overlooked the growing tendency of the public sector to imitate the private. For decades management techniques, including records management, have been borrowed from commerce and in the 1980s a further impetus has been given to that process by central government's determination to achieve 'value for money' from local services in a commercial sense. Local authorities are being encouraged to make a radical scrutiny of their activities and to reappraise traditional notions of funding. Some are seeking private sponsorship for projects or undertaking joint ventures with commercial firms. Others are establishing trading companies to sell goods and services to the public and, under the Highways Act 1980 and the Local Government Act 1988, direct labour organisations and direct service organisations are being set up to bid against commercial firms for certain council services which are open to competitive tendering. Although these companies, since they use public funds, operate under certain constraints, they are established on the mercantile model; the local government records manager can no longer afford to ignore the Companies Acts. It remains to be seen whether contact with the market-place will transform the professional, low-key, low-tech, conservative, archive-dominated records management services described here into something more like their commercial counterparts.

Further reading on local government

Cook, M., *Archive Administration*, Dawson, 1977.
Knightbridge, A. A. H., *Archive Legislation in the United Kingdom*, Society of Archivists Information Leaflet 3, 1985.
The Records of Education Departments, Records Management Group, Society of Archivists, 1987.
The Records of Social Services Departments, Records Management Group, Society of Archivists, 1988.

SELECT BIBLIOGRAPHY

In addition to the works cited specifically in the text, the following books will provide valuable additional information and guidance.

Benedon, W. (1969) *Records Management*, New Jersey: Prentice Hall.

British Standards Institution (1975) *Recommendations for the Processing and Storage of Silver Gelatine Type Microfilm*, BS 1153, London.

British Standards Institution (1984) *Guide to the Preparation of Microfilm and other Microforms that may be Required in Evidence*, BS 6498, London.

Cook, M. (1977) *Archives Administration*, Folkestone: Dawson & Co.

Cook, M. (1986) *The Management of Information from Archives*, London: Gower Press.

Cook, M. (ed.) (1987) *Computer Generated Records*, London: Society of Archivists.

Diamond, S. Z. (1983) *Records Management: A Practical Guide*, New York: ACCOM.

Emmerson, P. (1984) *Records Retention*, London: Business Archives Council, Records Aids No. 3.

Hedstrom, M. L. (1984) *Archives and Manuscripts: Machine Readable Records*, Chicago: Society of American Archivists, Basic Manual Series.

Leahy, E. J. and Cameron, C. A. (1965) *Modern Records Management*, New York: McGraw-Hill.

McCarthy, J. D. (1983) *Records Management in Business*, London: Business Archives Council, Records Aids No. 1.

Meadke, W. O., Brown, G. F. and Robek, M. F. (1987) *Information and Records Management* (3rd edn), New York: Glencoe Publishing.

Morddel, A., Penn, I., Pennix, G. and Smith, K. (1989) *A Records Management Handbook*, London: Gower Press.

Newton, S. C. (ed.) (1981) *Office Automation and Records Management*, London: Society of Archivists Records Management Group.

Newton, S. C. (1984) *Strategic Planning for Records Management*, London: Society of Archivists Records Management Group.

Place, I. and Hyslop, D. J. (1982) *Records Management: Controlling Business Information*, New York: Reston.

Ricks, B. R. and Gow, K. F. (1984) *Information Resource Management*, Cincinnati: South Western Publishing Co.

Schellenberg, T. R. (1956) *Modern Archives: Principles and Techniques*, Chicago: University of Chicago Press. (Midway reprint 1975.)

Southwood, G. (1988) *Storing Current Records Efficiently*, London: H.M. Treasury.

Waegemann, C. P. (1988) *Handbook of Records Storage and Space Management*, Westport, Conn.: Quorum books.

There are a number of useful journals in the field which carry detailed technical articles on the subjects covered in general in the above books. In particular, see the following:

Business Archives: Principles and Practice, Business Archives Council
Information Media and Technology, National Centre for Information Media and Technology (CIMTECH)
International Records Management Journal, International Records Management Council
Records Management Bulletin, Records Management Society
Records Management Quarterly, Association of Records Managers and Administrators Inc., USA

Reference should also be made to the publications of the following bodies:

ASLIB, The Association for Information Management
Association of Records Managers and Administrators Inc. USA
British Computer Society
Business Archives Council
Centre for Information Media and Technology
Institute of Information Scientists
International Records Management Council
Records Management Society
Society of Archivists Records Management Group

INDEX